DO YOU REMEMBER?

THE 1940s

An exclusive edition for

ALLSORTED.
for all your gift books and gift stationery

Watford, Herts, U.K. WD19 4BG

for all your gift books and gift stationery

Published in 2016 by Allsorted. Watford, Herts, U.K. WD19 4BG

Compiled by Michael Powell
Illustrations reproduced courtesy of Shutterstock.com
Concept by Milestone Design
Designed by Joanna Ross at Double Fish Design Ltd

Printed in China

Introduction

The forties were remarkable. Well, you should know because you lived through them. This special decade witnessed the first long-playing phonograph record, the last execution at the Tower of London and did you know that in 1943 a pint of beer cost the equivalent of just five pence today?

You could hear Anne Shelton, Duke Ellington and Vera Lynn on the radio and watch Audie Murphy, Katharine Hepburn and Humphrey Bogart on the big screen. Wolverhampton Wanderers won the FA Cup, Hitler was defeated and penicillin went into mass production. What a great time to be growing up.

Well, that was all a long time ago, but you'd be surprised how many memories you can refresh with a little encouragement. There are fifty-four quizzes and more than 1,000 questions covering world events, music, films, celebrities, fads and crazes, fashions, comedians, actors, singers, inventions, advertisements, novels, toys, sporting greats, scientific achievements and lots of things that made your forties childhood unique.

Some of the questions will be easy for you to answer but almost impossible for those without your personal experience. Other questions will call up random memories to make you smile. All those real moments have disappeared but you will always have this book to remind you!

Contents

Contents

The Year That Was

1940

1. On 17th January, which British river froze for the first time since 1888?

2. On 3rd February, how did a Heinkel He 111 bomber make history?

3. Disguised in battleship grey, which ocean liner began her maiden voyage from Clydebank to New York on 3rd March?

4. On 29th March, what was added to £1 notes to thwart forgeries?

5. On 10th May, who resigned as British Prime Minister?

6. On 13th May, which European monarch was evacuated to London aboard HMS *Hereward*?

7. On 9th June, what elite British force was created to perform raids into German occupied territory?

8. Which country declared war on France and the United Kingdom on 10th June?

9. Which European city fell to the Germans on 14th June?

10. On 17th June, which British troopship was bombed and sunk by the Luftwaffe with the loss of more than 4,000 lives?

11. On 23rd June, which BBC Forces non-stop popular/light music daytime radio programme was broadcast for the first time?

12. What pivotal event of WWII began on 10th July?

13. On 21st August, which exiled Russian revolutionary was assassinated with an ice axe outside Mexico City?

14. From 7th September, which British city was bombed by the Luftwaffe for 57 consecutive nights?

15. On 12th September, the entrance to the Lascaux caves was discovered near the village of Montignac in South West France. What is their archaeological significance?

16. On 23rd September, King George VI announced the introduction of which military decoration?

17. Which member of The Beatles was born on 9th October?

18. On 14th October, at which London Underground station were at least 64 people killed by a German bomb?

19. Which industrial city of the West Midlands suffered its most devastating bombing attacks on 14th November?

20. On 31st December, as London burned, the front page of the *Daily Mail* displayed a photo of which famous London landmark intact, below the caption 'WAR'S GREATEST PICTURE'?

The Year That Was

1941

1. Which member of *Monty Python's Flying Circus* was born in Leicester on 8th January?

2. On 22nd January, Australian and British forces captured this strategically important port city on Libya's Eastern Mediterranean coast.

3. On 19th February, 3 nights of German bombing began, causing 230 deaths in which city in South Wales?

4. On 11th March, President Franklin D. Roosevelt signed the Lend-Lease Act. What did it authorise the United States to do?

5. On 6th April, Germany invaded Yugoslavia and which other European country?

6. On 9th May, how did the Royal Navy acquire a German Enigma cryptography machine and its codebooks?

7. On 10th May, Hitler's deputy parachuted into Scotland in an attempt to begin peace talks. What was his name?

8. On 24th May, which iconic Royal Navy battlecruiser was sunk in the North Atlantic by the German battleship *Bismarck*?

9. Which German battleship was sunk by the Royal Navy on 27th May, 1941?

10. Operation Barbarossa, which began on 22nd June, was the code name for the German invasion of which country?

11. In July, which British regiment was formed by David Stirling?

12. On 9th August, which RAF flying ace was taken prisoner by the Germans after bailing out of his plane over France and was subsequently sent to Colditz Castle?

13. On 15th August, a German spy became the last person to be executed at the Tower of London. What was his name?

14. German forces began a prolonged military blockade of which important Baltic Sea port on 8th September?

15. On 11th September, construction began on which American military building in Arlington County, Virginia?

16. Walt Disney released his fourth animated film on 23rd October. What was its name?

17. On 13th November, this iconic aircraft carrier was torpedoed by a German submarine off Gibraltar.

18. On 5th December, Britain declared war on Hungary, Romania and which Nordic country?

19. On 7th December, the Imperial Japanese Navy launched a surprise attack on Pearl Harbor, which is in which United States Territory?

20. In Washington, D.C. on 27th December, Winston Churchill became the first British Prime Minister to do what?

The Year That Was

1942

1. In January, a major hoard of highly decorative Roman silver tableware from the fourth-century AD was discovered in Suffolk. What is its name?

2. On 8th January, which famous British physicist was born in Oxford?

3. The Sikorsky R-4 made its maiden flight on 13th January and went on to become the first vehicle of its kind to be mass-produced. What was it?

4. Which Hollywood actress was killed on 16th January when her plane crashed near Las Vegas while she was on a tour selling war bonds?

5. On 29th January, *Desert Island Discs* was first broadcast and the star of the radio show *Hi, Gang!* was its castaway. What was his name?

6. On 25th February, which member of the Royal Family registered for war service?

7. On 16th March, New Zealand and Australia declared war on which country on Southeast Asia's Indochinese Peninsula?

8. On 20th March, which song from the film *Holiday Inn*, won the

Academy Award for Best Original Song?

9. On 15th April, King George VI awarded the George Cross to which besieged archipelago in the Central Mediterranean?

10. On 23rd April, William Temple was enthroned in which British diocesan office?

11. During the spring, two Nazi German extermination camps opened in occupied Poland. What were their names?

12. On 21st May, following the sinking of the tanker *Faja de Oro* by a German submarine, which country declared war on Germany?

13. On 12th June, Anne Frank received a diary for her 13th birthday and made her first entry. In which European city was she living?

14. The Oxford Committee for Famine Relief was founded on 31st July. By what name is it commonly known?

15. On 8th August, Walt Disney's fifth animated film had its world premiere in London. What was its title?

16. On 11th August in London, which new bridge was opened to traffic to cross the River Thames?

17. On 25th August, which member of the Royal Family was killed in an air crash near Caithness, Scotland?

18. On 2nd October, the British cruiser HMS *Curacao* sank with the loss of 338 lives after colliding with which ocean liner off the coast of Donegal?

19. On 25th October, which drink ration was reduced to two and a half pints a week?

20. On 1st December, an influential report on Social Insurance and Allied Services was published, which would later form the basis for the welfare state. By what name is it commonly known?

The Year That Was

1943

1. Churchill and Roosevelt began a conference in which Moroccan city on 14th January?

2. On 15th January in Arlington County, Virginia, the largest office building in the world was dedicated. What is its name?

3. On 2nd February, the German 6th Army surrendered to Russia on the Eastern Front at the end of which major battle?

4. Between 10th February and 3rd March, which independence leader maintained a hunger strike in protest of his imprisonment by the British?

5. On 3rd March, the worst civilian disaster of WWII occurred, when 183 lives were lost in a crush during an air raid on which London tube station?

6. On 4th March, who made an acceptance speech for the Academy Award for Best Actress that was a record-breaking six minutes long?

7. Which box office smash Rodgers and Hammerstein musical, originally titled *Away We Go!*, opened on Broadway on 31st March?

8. On 16th and 17th May, which squadron of the RAF used bouncing bombs to destroy German dams in the Ruhr Valley?

9. What was the name of the American Boeing B-17F Flying Fortress that in May became the first to complete 25 combat missions unscathed?

10. On 3rd June, in which American city did the Zoot Suit Riots begin?

11. Which *Doctor Who* actor was born on 8th June?

12. On 17th July, which Italian city suffered major bombing for the first time?

13. On 25th July, which Fascist Prime Minister was deposed and arrested?

14. On 26th August, this British statesman and uncle of Prince Philip, Duke of Edinburgh was appointed Supreme Allied Commander for Southeast Asia.

15. On 14th October, an uprising allowed the escape of half the inmates of which Nazi extermination camp?

16. On 18th October, Chiang Kai-shek became the Chairman of the Nationalist Government of which country?

17. On 28th November, the so-called 'Big Three' met at the Tehran Conference. Who were they?

18. On 2nd December, the first of 48,000 young British conscripts were sent to work in the coal mines. What was their collective nickname?

19. On 2nd December, White Vision, Winkie and Tyke were the first recipients of the Dickin Medal (the animal equivalent of the Victoria Cross). What kind of animals were they?

20. After 14 years, what officially ended in the US on 4th December thanks to wartime employment?

The Year That Was

1944

1. On 9th January, the founder and guitarist of Led Zeppelin was born in London. What is his name?

2. The Battle of Monte Cassino began on 17th January in which European country?

3. On 10th February, a new system of taxation was introduced in the UK. By what four-letter acronym is it commonly known?

4. On 2nd March, which romantic film set in Morocco and directed by Michael Curtiz won the Academy Award for Best Picture?

5. From 10th March, married women were permitted by law to pursue which profession?

6. On 15th March, which Nordic country legalized same-sex sexual activity?

7. On 18th March, 26 people were killed by the last eruption of a volcano in the Campania region of Italy? What is its name?

8. How did RAF Flight Sergeant Nicholas Alkemade narrowly escape death on 20th March?

9. What is 'Harry' and how did it enable the escape of 76 Royal Air Force prisoners of war from Stalag Luft III on the night of 24th March?

10. What part did the Paul Verlaine poem *Chanson d'automne* play on 5th June, the eve of The Normandy Landings?

11. On 6th June, The Normandy Landings began. What was the operational code name?

12. The doodlebug reached London for the first time on 13th June. What was its official name?

13. On 16th June, 14-year-old African-American George Stinney became the youngest person in the twentieth century in the United States to undergo what?

14. On 17th June, which Nordic island country declared full independence from Denmark?

15. On 20th July, Claus von Stauffenberg led an unsuccessful assassination attempt. Who was his target?

16. On 3rd August, The Education Act transformed secondary education in England and Wales by creating what three types of schools?

17. Who was the Conservative education minister who oversaw this change?

18. On 12th August, British engineers laid the first undersea oil pipeline which ran between England and France under the code name acronym PLUTO. What does it stand for?

19. On 8th September, the first V-2 rocket hit London. What does its German name *Vergeltungswaffe 2* mean in English?

20. On 12th October, Henry Larsen became the first person to navigate in both directions the sea route that connects the Atlantic and Pacific Oceans through the Arctic Ocean? What is its name?

The Year That Was

1945

1. Which celebrated English cellist was born in Jersey on 26th January?

2. On 4th February, Winston Churchill, President Franklin D. Roosevelt and Joseph Stalin met at the Yalta Conference, located on which peninsular on the north coast of the Black Sea?

3. On 23rd February, Joe Rosenthal took a Pulitzer Prize winning photograph of a group of United States Marines on the island of Iwo Jima doing what?

4. On 10th March, 67 German prisoners of war escaped from Island Farm Camp located at this Welsh town, 20 miles east of Swansea.

5. In April, the barrister Sybil Campbell was the first woman in the UK to become a full-time professional what?

6. On 15th April, British troops liberated a concentration camp in Northern Germany. What was its name?

7. On 30th April, Adolf Hitler took his own life in his Führerbunker in Berlin. How?

8. On 5th May, which pro-Fascist American poet was arrested by American forces and imprisoned for treason?

9. On 9th May, German forces in the only occupied part of the United Kingdom surrendered. Where were they?

10. On 28th May, William Joyce was captured and tried for treason for his radio broadcasts. By what name is he best remembered?

11. On 5th July, what took place in the UK for the first time in ten years?

12. On 16th July, The Trinity Test took place in the Jornada del Muerto Desert, New Mexico to test 'The Gadget'. What was it?

13. On 28th July, who became the new British Prime Minister?

14. The BBC launched a new music and light entertainment radio station on 29th July. What was its original name and what is it called today?

15. On 5th August, which family cartoon first appeared in the *Sunday Express*?

16. On 6th August, the *Enola Gay* dropped an atomic bomb on Hiroshima. What was the bomb's diminutive code name?

17. Referencing the forthcoming Cold War, which two-word metaphorical phrase did Winston Churchill use in the House of Commons for the first time on 16th August?

18. On 17th August, Indian born ex-Etonian Eric Blair published an allegorical anti-Soviet novella. By what pen name is he better known?

19. On 2nd October, which London Underground station was the first to use fluorescent lighting?

20. On 31st December, which fruit appeared in Britain for the first time since the beginning of the war?

The Year That Was

1946

1. On 10th January, which newly formed intergovernmental organisation held its first meeting in Methodist Central Hall Westminster in London?

2. On 10th January, Project Diana used radar waves to measure the precise distance between which two objects?

3. Who resigned as head of the French provisional government on 20th January?

4. In February, the first programmable, electronic digital computer was installed at the University of Pennsylvania. What was its name?

5. On 24th February, Juan Perón was elected president of which South American country?

6. In which island country in East Asia did women vote for the first time on 10th April?

7. On 23rd April, the Piaggio company took out a patent on a stylish new vehicle whose name means 'wasp' in Italian. What was it?

8. Burt Lancaster starred in two films that were inspired by the events of 2nd May, when six inmates tried to escape from which American Federal Penitentiary?

9. On 7th May, Tokyo Telecommunications Engineering was founded with about 20 employees. By what name is it known today?

10. On 26th May, a patent was filed in the US for which weapon?

11. On 31st May, which European country voted in a referendum to return its king, George II?

12. On 13th June, King Umberto II went into exile in Portugal after which country was declared a republic?

13. Which international film festival was founded in this year?

14. Which item of beachwear first went on sale in Paris on 5th July?

15. Which flag carrier airline was founded in Hong Kong on 24th September?

16. The high IQ organisation Mensa was founded on 1st October and took its name from the Latin word for which piece of furniture?

17. On 2nd October, Illinois Bell Telephone Company launched the world's first what?

18. Which Hollywood actress and star of the films *The Rocky Horror Picture Show* (1975) and *Dead Man Walking* (1995) was born on 4th October?

19. Which puppet with his 'friend' Annette Mills made his television debut on *For the Children*, broadcast by the BBC on 20th October?

20. On 11th December, the international humanitarian programme UNICEF was founded. What is its full name?

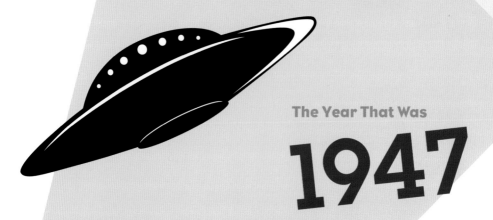

The Year That Was

1947

1. From 2nd January, which precious metal was no longer included in British coins?

2. Which English singer and songwriter was born David Jones in Brixton, South London on 8th January?

3. Which famous Chicago crime boss died on 25th January at his mansion in Palm Island, Florida?

4. On 10th February, why was BBC Television suspended until 11th March?

5. On 20th February, which Earl became the last Viceroy of India?

6. On 20th February, Ealing Studios released the film *Hue and Cry*. It was the first what?

7. On 22nd February, the animated cartoon *Cat Fishin'* was released. It was the 27th short film to star which pair of characters?

8. On 1st April, what was raised to age 15?

9. The BBC first broadcast the radio programme *How Does Your Garden Grow?* on 9th April. What is it called today?

10. Which German archipelago in the North Sea was used as a British bombing range and was nearly obliterated when the Royal Navy detonated 6,700 tonnes of explosive on 18th April?

11. Which Swedish former aerospace company produced its first prototype car on 10th June?

12. From 11th–15th June, which international cultural event was held for the first time?

13. Which famous couple announced their engagement on 10th July?

14. In Scotland, which international cultural event was held for the first time on 31st August?

15. On 8th July, the headline of the *Roswell Daily Record*

in New Mexico announced the capture of what?

16. On 7th August, Thor Heyerdahl ended his 4,300-mile voyage across the Eastern Pacific Ocean. What was the name of his balsa wood raft?

17. October witnessed the first recorded use of which word that describes an electronic digital machine?

18. On 12th November, how did Chancellor of the Exchequer Hugh Dalton get himself the sack?

19. What televised event on 20th November was viewed by an estimated 400,000 people in Britain?

20. On 6th December, which British university allowed women to become full students?

The Year That Was

1948

1. In January, what popular new shopping system did Marks & Spencer trial in the food section of their Wood Green store in London?

2. On 5th January, the first episode of *Mrs Dale's Diary* was broadcast on the BBC Light Programme. Who played the eponymous doctor's wife?

3. On 17th January, Manchester United and Arsenal drew at Maine Road in front of 83,260 spectators. What was special about this game?

4. Which independence activist was assassinated at the age of 78 on 30th January?

5. On 17th March, Britain signed the Treaty of Brussels with Belgium, France and which two other European countries?

6. On 23rd March, the BBC first broadcast the radio comedy *Take It From Here*. Which comedy duo wrote the scripts?

7. Which distinctive mint sweets were introduced by Rowntree on 15th April?

8. Which British workhorse debuted at the Amsterdam Motor Show on 30th April?

9. On 14th May, David Ben-Gurion became the leader of which newly formed independent state?

10. What was the name of the relief effort that began on 26th June to help the people of West Berlin?

11. On 1st July, the Welsh Folk Museum opened in which western area of the city of Cardiff?

12. The Labour government implemented the recommendations of The Beveridge Report by launching this publicly funded system in the UK on 5th July.

13. On 15th July, the first London chapter of which alliterative international mutual aid fellowship met?

14. On 18th August, the nation's first what opened in Potters Bar and Hillingdon?

15. At Haydock Park Racecourse on 18th August, a 12-year-old jockey won the first race of his illustrious career. What was his name?

16. On 6th September, John Derry became the first test pilot to do what?

17. The BBC Home Service broadcast *Any Questions* for the first time on 12th October. Who was its first host?

18. How did Princess Elizabeth excite an expectant nation on 14th November?

19. Which British philosopher delivered the first series of Reith Lectures on 26th December on the BBC Home Service?

20. The first person to drive a car faster than 300 mph died in Reigate, Surrey on 31st December, aged 63. What was his name?

The Year That Was

1949

1. Which children's character did Enid Blyton introduce this year: Brer Rabbit, Noddy or Amelia Jane?

2. From 1st January, all men aged 18–26 in England, Scotland and Wales were obliged to spend 18 months doing what?

3. During an appearance on BBC radio on 28th March, which two-word phrase did astronomer Fred Hoyle introduce into the English lexicon while discussing the formation of the Universe?

4. On 1st April, which British privately-owned stately home in Southwest England was the first to open its doors to the paying public?

5. What treaty was signed by Britain and 11 other nations on 4th April to protect territorial integrity, political independence and security?

6. On 20th April, which sporting event was held for the first time at Badminton House in Gloucestershire?

7. On 30th April, which football team won the FA Cup Final for the first time in 41 years?

8. On 1st May, Dutch-American astronomer Gerard Kuiper discovered the moon Nereid orbiting which planet in our solar system?

9. On 9th May, the first self-service facility of its kind in the country opened in Queensway, London. What was it?

10. What was the name of the Ealing Comedy film released on 16th June, based on the real-life tale of a shipwreck near the Scottish island of Eriskay?

11. On 27th July, a British-built de Havilland DH 106 Comet made its maiden flight. It was the world's first what?

12. The Fourth Geneva Convention was adopted in August. It defined humanitarian protection during war for which group of people?

13. On 29th August, the Soviet Union tested 'Joe 1', its first what?

14. Which sixties icon and fashion model was born Lesley Hornby on 19th September?

15. On 29th September, Iva Toguri D'Aquino was found guilty of broadcasting Japanese radio propaganda in the South Pacific during World War II. What was her floral nickname?

16. Physician and former Rector of the University of Glasgow, John Boyd Orr, received the Nobel Peace Prize on 12th October for his scientific research into improvements in the production of what?

17. The first comedy series on British television, *How Do You View?*, debuted on 26th October, showcasing the gap-toothed grin of which famous English comedian?

18. Which Monmouthshire town became the first New Town in Wales on 4th November?

19. The BBC opened its first regional transmitting station on 17th December in which English Midlands town?

20. On 27th December, following four years of intermittent but bloody conflict, Indonesia finally gained its independence from which European country?

The Forces' Sweethearts

Betty Grable

1. How old was she when she made her illegal screen debut as a chorus girl in the 1929 film, *Happy Days*?

2. During her late teens she appeared in *The Gay Divorcee* and which nautical-themed musical that also starred Fred Astaire and Ginger Rogers?

3. She suffered from demophobia – the fear of what?

4. She had the most expensively insured legs in show business. What was her nickname?

5. Name the 'undisputed First Lady of the musical comedy stage' with whom Betty starred on Broadway in the Cole Porter musical *DuBarry Was a Lady*.

6. Soon afterwards she was spotted by Darryl F. Zanuck, the head of which Hollywood film studio?

7. Zanuck immediately cast her in the lavish Technicolor musical film *Down Argentine Way* with Don Ameche and which Brazilian bombshell?

8. Name the black-and-white film noir in which she starred with Victor Mature as the sister of a young murdered model.

9. Which actor co-starred with her in both *Song of the Islands* and *Footlight Serenade*?

10. In 1942, she starred in *Springtime in the Rockies* with a trumpet-playing bandleader whom she later married. What was his name?

11. Her next film, *Coney Island*, was a period musical set during which decadent decade of the nineteenth century?

12. In 1943, photographer Frank Powolny took an iconic multi-million selling photo in which she wore a white one-piece bathing suit and struck what famous pose?

13. What was the name of the 1944 film that cashed in on her pin-up status?

14. Name her box office hit that was released in 1947 and was framed through several flashbacks of two ageing vaudeville performers.

15. Name the actor who co-starred with Grable in the 1948 film *That Lady in Ermine*, and who is remembered for his brief marriage to Joan Crawford almost 20 years earlier.

16. Her next hit was the musical film *When My Baby Smiles at Me*, one of four films in which she co-starred with which American dancer and actor?

17. Despite being one of the highest paid stars in the world, in which 1953 film – also starring Jane Russell – was she replaced by Marilyn Monroe because she demanded too much money?

18. One of her biggest successes was a romantic comedy in which she, Marilyn Monroe and Lauren Bacall plotted to find wealthy husbands. What was its title?

19. Grable was replaced by Ethel Merman after she turned down which 1954 Irving Berlin musical whose title is also a song in the musical *Annie Get Your Gun*?

20. Name the 1955 film in which she made her final big screen appearance: *The Farmer Takes a Wife*, *Three for the Show* or *How to Be Very, Very Popular*?

Major Inventions

of the Decade

1. The Aqua-Lung was invented by two Frenchmen: Émile Gagnan and a naval lieutenant who found fame as an underwater documentary filmmaker. What was his name?

2. In 1943, Dutch physician Willem Kolff developed a machine designed to perform the function of which body organ?

3. In 1945, which household appliance was invented by accident when Percy Spencer noticed that a chocolate bar in his pocket had melted?

4. In 1948, Walter Frederick Morrison and his partner Warren Franscioni invented a plastic disc called the 'Flying Saucer'. By what name is it more commonly known?

5. In 1941, Lyle Goodhue and William Sullivan developed a dispensing system dubbed the 'bug bomb'. Today, several can be found in nearly every modern home. What is it?

6. In 1941, at the Radcliffe Infirmary in Oxford the first ever clinical trials were carried out for which popular medication?

7. During World War II, engineer James Wright accidentally created a non-Newtonian fluid that became one of the best-selling toys of the twentieth century. What is its name?

8. In February 1944, the prototype, Colossus Mark I became operational at Bletchley Park in Buckinghamshire. It was the world's first what?

9. What is the name of the hook and loop technology that Swiss engineer and amateur mountaineer George de Mestral invented while hiking with his dog in the Jura Mountains?

10. Which chocolate-covered sweets were first made in 1942 for American soldiers in WWII?

11. On 16th April, 1943, Swiss chemist Albert Hofmann discovered powerful effects of Lysergic acid diethylamide. What is its common name?

12. Which metal children's toy sprang to fame in the US in 1946?

13. Which invention shook the world on 6th August and 9th August, 1945?

14. In 1947, Danish carpenter Ole Kirk Christiansen purchased his country's first plastic moulding machine. What toy did he produce?

15. Earl Silas Tupper's airtight invention first went on sale in 1948. What was it?

16. Which iconic word-based board game was invented during the Great Depression, but was not trademarked until 1948?

17. In 1947, American physicists John Bardeen, Walter Brattain and William Shockley developed a semiconductor device that revolutionised the field of electronics. By what name is it commonly known?

18. On 16th August, 1944, which Scottish inventor gave the world's first demonstration of a fully electronic colour television?

19. Name the Scottish pharmacologist who shared the 1945 Nobel Prize in Medicine with Howard Florey and Ernst Chain.

20. The Germans named their wartime invention the *Wehrmachtskanister*. What is it called in English?

Big Bands

1. American bandleader Harry James had a 1941 hit with 'You Made Me Love You' and was the first to hire which future 'bobby soxer' idol?

2. Which big band leader shared his name with a British post-war Prime Minister?

3. English bandleader Solomon Schwartz was conductor of the BBC Dance Orchestra for nine years and was one of the most-heard musicians on the radio. By what colourful name is he better known?

4. 'One O'Clock Jump' was the theme song for whose big band: Billy Cotton, Count Basie or Benny Goodman?

5. Whose melodic trombone playing and the huge hit, 'Opus One' made his orchestra one of the most popular of the swing era?

6. On 10th February, 1942, RCA Victor presented Glenn Miller with the very first what for his hit 'Chattanooga Choo-Choo'?

7. Whose biggest hit was the eponymous up-tempo blues number 'Woodchopper's Ball'?

8. Who started his radio show with the cry 'Wakey-Wake-aaaay!', followed by his signature tune 'Somebody Stole My Gal'?

BIG BANDS

9. The original King of Swing, he grew up in Chicago's impoverished Jewish ghetto and had a massive hit with 'Sing, Sing, Sing'. What was his name?

10. American jazz pianist and bebop pioneer, Earl Hines, gave which legendary saxophonist his big break and subsequently fired him for poor timekeeping?

11. Which Duke Ellington classic encouraged travellers to ride the New York Subway from Eastern Brooklyn up into Harlem and Northern Manhattan?

12. Which Lancashire born bandleader and impresario is known for his signature tune 'Oh Listen to the Band' and for re-forming The Crazy Gang show?

13. Who had the theme song 'Artistry in Rhythm' and was the father of former beauty editor of *Harpers & Queen*, Leslie Kenton?

14. Which American bandleader died on 15th December, 1944 aged 40 when his plane went missing over the English Channel?

15. What was unusual about Ivy Benson's big swing band?

16. Which millionaire playboy was nicknamed 'Mad Mab' and had a hit with 'Cherokee'?

17. Which stellar Hoagy Carmichael classic, played by Artie Shaw and his orchestra, is widely considered to be the supreme big band recording of all time?

18. Which English singer, drummer and bandleader is best known for providing the musical interludes on *The Goon Show*?

19. The telephone number of the Hotel Pennsylvania in New York was the inspiration for which Glenn Miller hit?

20. Which word, more recently popularised by the *Harry Potter* books, was a slang term for marijuana amongst jazz musicians of the 1920s and 1930s?

George Formby

1. He was born in 1904 in which Lancashire town?

2. He was blind for the first few weeks of his life. How was his sight restored?

3. During his childhood he was apprenticed to which sport?

4. His real name was George Hoy Booth. Where did he get the idea for his stage name?

5. He spent two years struggling to make a living as an entertainer until he introduced what into his act?

6. Which signature song did Formby debut in the 1936 British comedy film *Keep Your Seats, Please*?

7. His manager wife, Beryl, had a successful music-hall act doing what?

8. Which 1937 hit was banned by the BBC during the forties because of its suggestive lyrics?

9. In 1940, he took part in a show for the BBC that was broadcast under the banner 'Let the People Sing', for which organisation?

10. In May 1941, he performed for the Royal Family at Windsor Castle and decided to sing the original, uncensored version of which signature song?

11. In which 1941 film did he play George Pearson, an employee at an underwear factory?

12. According to his hit song, what was George doing at the corner of the street, 'in case a certain little lady comes by'?

13. He became the highest paid entertainer in Britain after signing a six-film deal with Columbia Pictures for: £65,000, £100,000 or £500,000?

14. Who co-starred with him in the 1942 film *Much Too Shy* and is best remembered as the London East End charwoman, Mrs Huggett?

15. His co-star in the 1943 film *Get Cracking* is also known for the roles of Wendy McKim in the comedy *Genevieve* (1953) and as the mother in *The Railway Children* (1970). What was her name?

16. Name the 1940 film in which George plays a bumbling wartime policeman who becomes a hero after he saves HMS *Hercules*.

17. Name the 1944 film whose title is a pun on a famous Oliver Goldsmith comedy of manners, *She Stoops to Conquer*.

18. Formby toured abroad extensively with ENSA and performed to an estimated: 1 million, 3 million or 5 million troops?

19. In 1946, he returned to the music hall after his final film flopped at the box office? What was its title?

20. Towards the end of the decade he briefly became addicted to which analgesic and narcotic drug?

The Forces' Sweethearts

Rita Hayworth

1. What was her birth name: Margarita Cansino, Birgita Schneider or Rita Worthington?

2. Where did she find the inspiration to change her name to Hayworth?

3. She was a supporting cast member on the 1940 comedy-drama *Susan and God*, which starred the actress once described by *Life* magazine as the first 'Queen of the Movies'. What was her name?

4. In 1941, she played the second female lead in *The Strawberry Blonde* opposite James Cagney.

Who was the female star?

5. She played the socialite Dona Sol in *Blood and Sand*. Which actor played Juan, the Spanish bullfighter who falls under her spell?

6. Which leading male dancer of the era considered her to be his favourite dancing partner?

7. What was her nickname: The Love Goddess, First Lady of the American Screen or The Red She-Devil?

8. Name the film in which she performed a legendary one-glove striptease.

9. Who was her dancing partner in the Hollywood musicals *You'll Never Get Rich* (1941) and *You Were Never Lovelier* (1942)?

10. In *My Gal Sal* (1942) she played a musical star called Sally Elliott in Gay Nineties New York. Which hard-boiled heavy-lidded hunk was her co-star?

11. Which film star/director did Hayworth marry on 7th September, 1943 and consider the love of her life?

12. How many times did she marry and divorce?

13. What was the title of her huge 1944 hit Technicolor musical with Gene Kelly?

14. Her 1945 musical *Tonight and Every Night* is loosely based around a real London theatre that was famous for aiming never to miss a show during the Blitz. What was its name?

15. Who was the male lead in her 1946 film noir, *Gilda*?

16. In 1946, she was horrified when she learned that her bombshell status meant that scientists on the Marshall Islands had stuck her photograph on what?

17. Complete this song lyric: 'Put the blame on _____.'

18. The box office failure of the 1947 Orson Welles film, *The Lady from Shanghai*, has been blamed in part for her cutting her hair short and dyeing it what colour?

19. In 1948, she left Hollywood to marry the son of a Sultan, Prince Aly Khan. She filed for divorce after he was spotted in a nightclub with which Academy Award-winning Alfred Hitchcock actress?

20. Name the 1953 Biblical epic film in which she played the titular role alongside Charles Laughton and Stewart Granger.

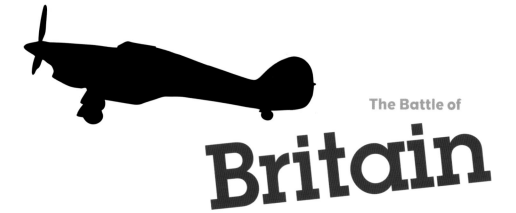

The Battle of

Britain

1. The Battle of Britain was a pivotal air campaign fought over Southern England during which months of 1940?

2. Which British politician effectively named the Battle of Britain more than three weeks before it began?

3. The Germans were so convinced that Britain would quickly surrender that they began making what?

4. True or false: when the war started, the RAF had twice as many Spitfire Mk I planes as they had Hurricane Mk I?

5. What was the maximum speed of the Mk IIa series I Hurricanes: 156 mph, 224 mph or 342 mph?

6. What was the name of the principle German fighter plane?

7. How many belt-fed .303" (7.7mm) Browning guns were mounted in each wing of British fighter planes?

8. The Heinkel He III, Dornier Do 17 and Junkers Ju 88 were The Luftwaffe's primary what?

THE BATTLE OF BRITAIN

9. On the British side, what type of plane were the *Armstrong Whitworth Whitley*, the *Handley-Page Hampden* and the *Vickers Wellington*?

10. By the summer of 1940 approximately how many planes were being built in Britain each week: 60, 120 or 300?

11. When battle commenced, which commodity was in shorter supply: British planes or trained pilots?

12. According to The Royal Air Force roll of honour for the Battle of Britain, what was unusual about 595 of the pilots?

13. RADAR was instrumental to British success during the Battle of Britain. What does the acronym RADAR stand for?

14. What was the system – named after Fighter Command's Commander-in-Chief – that collated all information from Early Warning radar stations to create a real-time battle map?

15. What two targets did the Germans attack first?

16. For his brave actions on 16th August, 1940, Flight Lieutenant James Nicolson became Fighter Command's only recipient of what during WWII?

17. After two weeks of targeting Fighter Command Airfields, what critical tactical error did the Germans make?

18. What famous sentence did Churchill use to pay tribute to the nearly 3,000 men of the RAF who took part in the Battle of Britain?

19. Battle of Britain Day commemorates these men on which date of the year?

20. After failing to gain air superiority, Adolf Hitler postponed and then cancelled a planned invasion of Britain. What was its operational code name?

Dunkirk

1. What was the operational code name for the evacuation of Dunkirk?

2. Where does this name come from?

3. On which date did the evacuation begin?

4. How many days did it last?

5. How many vessels took part: 861, 933 or 1,257?

6. What was the role of British Vice Admiral Bertram Ramsay?

7. Churchill had been Prime Minister for how many weeks when the evacuation began?

8. What were the Dunkirk Moles?

9. Why were they so important?

10. Some of the ships travelled to Dunkirk from as far away as which self-governing Crown dependency in the Irish Sea?

11. What was special about the 14ft open-topped fishing boat called *Tamzine*, now in the Imperial War Museum?

12. An unspecified number of little boats also took part and earned what title?

13. A vessel called the *Medway Queen* made trips to Dunkirk and back and rescued 7,000 men. What type of ship was it?

14. On 29th May, why did Hitler make the tactical error of halting the German army advance on Dunkirk?

15. During the evacuation what was the significance of the British destroyers *Grafton, Grenade, Wakeful, Basilisk, Havant* and *Keith*?

16. The RAF lost 145 aircraft including at least 42 what?

17. Apart from Britain, France and Belgium, which two other nations took part in the evacuation?

18. Name the paddle steamer that took part in the Dunkirk evacuation and was involved in a fatal collision with *Bowbelle* on the River Thames in 1989?

19. Initially it was estimated that 45,000 men could be rescued in two days. How many British and allied soldiers were eventually evacuated from the beaches of Dunkirk: a) 128,245, b) 295,412 or c) 338,226?

20. Afterwards, who reminded the British people: 'We must be very careful not to assign to this deliverance the attributes of a victory. Wars are not won by evacuations.'

The Ministry of Information

WWII Slogans

Complete the following slogans:

1. Your courage your cheerfulness your resolution will bring _____.

2. Let your shopping help our _____. Plan your _____ to avoid waste.

3. Be careful what you say. You never know who's on the_____!

4. Three words to the whole nation: Go _____!

5. Let us go _____.

6. We could do with thousands more like you. Join the _____.

7. Don't do it Mother – leave the _____ where they are.

THE MINISTRY OF INFORMATION – WWII SLOGANS

8. Save kitchen waste to feed the
   _____.

9. Coughs and _____
   spread _____.

10. Hitler will send no warning – so
    always carry your
    _____.

11. Don't keep a _____. It
    might get into the enemy's
    hands.

12. Mothers, send them out
    _____.

13. _____ for victory.

14. Look before you sleep. All
    windows and inner doors
    _____. _____
    in buckets? _____ in
    buckets? _____, clothes
    and torch handy? Good Night!

15. Keep it under your
    _____. Careless
    _____ costs
    _____.

16. Go through your wardrobe.
    _____ and
    _____.

17. _____ in the blackout.

18. Better pot-luck with Churchill
    today than _____ under
    Hitler tomorrow. Don't waste
    _____!

19. Lend a hand on _____.

20. Keep _____ and
    _____.

Rationing

1. On 22nd September 1939, just three weeks after the outbreak of war, Britain introduced rationing of which important commodity?

2. On 8th January, 1940, butter and which other two items, were the first foods to be rationed?

3. Which was rationed first: eggs or meat?

4. How many ounces of butter was one adult allowed to buy per week during the war: two, four, eight or twelve?

5. How many ounces of sugar was one adult allowed to buy per week during the war: two, four, eight or twelve?

6. What was the colour of ration books for pregnant women, nursing mothers and children under five?

7. What was the colour of ration books for children between five and sixteen years of age?

8. What was the colour of ration books for most adults?

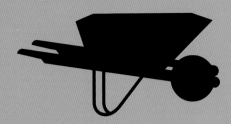

9. What was the name of the bespectacled and top hat clad vegetable billed by Ministry of Food advertisements as 'the children's best friend'?

10. What was the name of his tuberous companion?

11. Initially, how many clothing coupons were allocated to each person for a year: 20, 40, 60 or 80?

12. What staple food was prohibited after The Ministry of Food declared it lacked essential vitamins?

13. Which was rationed first: jam or cheese?

14. Which was rationed first: biscuits or sausages?

15. On 26th July 1942, rationing of sweets and chocolate began. How many ounces was each person allowed per week: one, two, four or eight?

16. What is a snook?

17. True or false: rationing for soap ended two years after rationing for tea?

18. A sealed packet of powdered egg stored in a cool dry place had a storage life of three, five or ten years?

19. Clothes rationing continued for how many years after the end of the war: two, four, six or nine?

20. In what year did food rationing end?

Victory in Europe Day

1. Which date was VE Day celebrated in the UK?

2. What day of the week was it?

3. When was news of German surrender transmitted on the BBC?

4. Following the suicide of Adolf Hitler, who succeeded him as the Nazi leader and authorised unconditional German surrender?

5. Mass crowds celebrated in which famous London square and along which road in the City of Westminster?

6. Who appeared on the balcony of Buckingham Palace with King George VI, Queen Elizabeth and the young princesses to wave to the cheering crowds?

7. How many times did the Royal Family appear on the balcony that day?

8. What celebratory item did The Board of Trade announce that people could buy without using ration coupons?

9. What did the huge crowd chant outside the gates of Buckingham Palace?

10. For many children VE Day was their first memory of eating which treat that had been banned since 1942?

11. How many consecutive thanksgiving services were held in St Paul's Cathedral on this day?

12. At what time did Winston Churchill address the nation?

13. What were built in their thousands across the country in a triumphant gesture ending six years of blackout?

14. One of the popular wartime songs that was sung throughout the nation begins, 'I give you a toast, ladies and gentleman'. What is its title?

15. Name four things that strangers did in the street!

16. In London, how did anti-aircraft searchlights play a part in the celebrations?

17. Which Hubert Gregg wartime doodlebug-inspired hit was also popular in London on this day?

18. After VE Day, many British troops were redeployed to the Far East and Pacific where war was still raging. How did they jokingly reword the acronym for the British Liberation Army (BLA) to reflect their tedious fate?

19. When did Japan sign its unconditional surrender and end the war?

20. Bombing stopped, war stopped but what continued for another nine years?

The 1948 Olympic Games

XIV TH OLYMPIAD

LONDON
1948

1. Due to the economic climate and post-war rationing, what nickname was given to these Games of the XIV Olympiad?

2. In which European city were they held?

3. How many years had it been since the previous Olympic Games?

4. Which two countries were refused permission to participate?

5. Which other large country stayed away?

6. The host was the second city to hold the games for a second time. Which was the first?

7. These were the first games to be held following the death of which famous French Baron?

8. Aside from his Olympian good looks, how is the British athlete John Mark best remembered?

9. Great Britain won three gold medals; two were for rowing and the third was for which other water sport?

10. Thirty-year-old Dutch mother of two, Fanny Blankers-Koen, won four gold medals for the 100m, 200m, 80m hurdles and 4x100m relay, earning her what nickname?

11. Over 90 per cent of all the competitors shared what in common?

12. Why were these games significant for Jamaica, Pakistan and Singapore?

13. This Olympiad saw the introduction of which sprint race innovation?

14. The Empire Olympic Pool housed 8,000 spectators and its construction made it the first facility of its kind in Olympic history. What was its unique appeal?

15. American athlete Bob Mathias won the gold medal for decathlon. Why was his victory unprecedented?

16. Ran Laurie and Jack Wilson won the gold medal for Rowing in the Men's Coxless Pairs. What is the name of Laurie's famous youngest son?

17. Laurie and Wilson's wartime posting in the Sudan Political Service earned them which rodentine nickname?

18. These Games included which contact team sport as a demonstration?

19. How much did the BBC pay for the broadcasting rights: £10 million, £1 million or 1,000 guineas?

20. For the lucky few who owned a television, how far away from the transmission station at Alexandra Palace in North London could they view the Games: 500, 250 or 25 miles?

The Forces' Sweethearts

Anne Shelton ♥

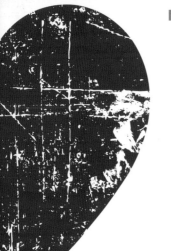

1. What was her maiden name: Patricia Sibley, Anne Shildon or Shelley-Anne Sheldon?

2. Anne started her career at the age of 13 and spent 6 years with which dance band, initially singing in her school uniform?

3. She was the original singer in the United Kingdom of the English version of which German love song?

4. The lyrics for this song were written by Tommie Connor, who is best remembered for which Jimmy Boyd Christmas hit?

5. In 1942–4 she appeared in the films *King Arthur was a Gentleman, Miss London Ltd.* and *Bees in Paradise* with which popular comedian?

6. Name her sister who sang with her on several occasions during her career?

7. What was the name of her radio show that ran for four years and was primarily aimed at soldiers serving in North Africa?

8. Her other popular BBC radio programme was broadcast from 1942 to 1947 and was a lifeline to troops serving on which Central Mediterranean archipelago?

THE FORCES' SWEETHEARTS – ANNE SHELTON

9. Which American big band arrived in England in 1944 and performed six shows with Anne?

10. In 1944, commitments in England forced her to turn down an offer of work across the English Channel. Why did this save her life?

11. On 27th August 1944, Anne recorded the *Variety Bandbox* radio show with which American crooner?

12. Anne recorded 'Would You Like to Swing on a Star' after it won the 1944 Academy Award for Best Song in which Bing Crosby musical comedy-drama film?

13. Which 1948 hit, composed by Dick Farrelly, contains the line 'Same old moon above, same old words of love'?

14. In 1949, Anne had two hits in the USA. One was 'Be Mine' and the other shares its name with a famous sea lough on the west coast of Ireland.

15. How many days were in the title of her 1956 song that reached No. 20 in the UK?

16. In 1956, she spent four weeks at No. 1 in the UK Singles Chart with this song. It was briefly banned by the BBC for fear it would demotivate British troops during the Suez Crisis.

17. In 1959, she released a version of the Andy Williams song that reached No. 2 in the UK. Which saint is mentioned in its title?

18. In 1961, her entry, 'I Will Light a Candle' came fourth in a qualifying heat in which BBC Television competition?

19. Which nautical song was Anne Shelton's last chart hit and Petula Clark's first?

20. Her recording of 'I'll Be Seeing You' appears in which 1979 John Schlesinger film starring Richard Gere?

White Christmas

Bing Crosby

1. He earned his nickname 'Bing' as a young child; it comes from a comic strip he enjoyed reading. What was its name?

2. In 1928, he had his first number one hit with which famous song from the musical *Show Boat*?

3. When he married his first wife in 1930, she was more famous than him. What was her name?

4. Which technological development was instrumental in shaping his smooth, intimate conversational singing style?

5. He named his eldest son Gary after which close friend and Hollywood actor?

6. He is the third-highest selling actor ever by movie tickets sold. John Wayne is second; and the first was nicknamed 'The King of Hollywood'. Who tops the list?

7. Name the 1942 Irving Berlin film in which he teamed up with Fred Astaire.

8. In what year did he release Irving Berlin's 'White Christmas', the biggest hit of his career?

9. Why did he have to re-record the song six years later?

10. He delayed his second marriage due to his affair with which future princess?

11. Crosby won an Academy Award for Best Actor for his role as Father Chuck O'Malley in which 1944 film?

12. Name the film in which he reprised the role the following year alongside Ingrid Bergman and was nominated again.

13. Name the film for which he received his third Academy Award nomination for playing an alcoholic has-been actor alongside Grace Kelly.

14. He starred with Bob Hope and which actress and former big band singer in six Road to... musical comedies between 1940 and 1952?

15. Name three of the Road to... destinations.

16. When Rosemary Clooney and Crosby were romantically paired in White Christmas, what was the age gap between them?

17. From the 1940s to the 1960s he owned 15 per cent of which American baseball team in Pennsylvania?

18. He narrated and recorded song vocals for 'The Legend of Sleepy Hollow' section of which 1949 Disney animated film?

19. Name the 1956 Cole Porter musical comedy film in which he co-starred with Grace Kelly and Frank Sinatra.

20. Late in his career he was offered the role of a famous TV detective but turned it down in favour of playing golf. What was the role?

Classic Forties Movies

1. Which Alfred Hitchcock film features Ingrid Bergman as the American daughter of a convicted Nazi spy?

2. In which 1944 film did a young Elizabeth Taylor star with Mickey Rooney in her breakthrough role?

3. The 1944 film *Mr Skeffington* starred Claude Rains in the long-suffering eponymous title role. Which actress received an Academy Award nomination for playing his wealthy socialite wife, Fanny?

4. Who wrote the screenplay for the 1945 classic *Brief Encounter*, based on his 1936 one-act play *Still Life*?

5. The American romantic comedy *The Philadelphia Story* starred James Stewart and which Bristol-born screen legend as Katharine Hepburn's alcoholic ex-husband, C.K. Dexter Haven?

6. Which 1940 Disney film contains the song 'When You Wish Upon a Star'?

7. In *It's a Wonderful Life*, the young George Bailey rescues his younger brother from a frozen pond and sustains what lifelong injury?

8. In which film noir did Lauren Bacall play the character of Vivian Rutledge?

9. Who played the beautiful teenage girl, Estella, in David Lean's 1946 film, *Great Expectations*?

10. In 1944, Ingrid Bergman won the Academy Award for Best Actress for her portrayal of Paula Alquist in which film?

11. Which Disney film was completed four hours before premiering in New York City on 13th November, 1940.

12. Which drama film, directed by John Ford, revived the career of Walter Pidgeon and controversially beat *Citizen Kane* to win the 1942 Academy Award for Best Picture?

13. Which 1942 American romantic drama set during World War II was based on the unproduced stage play, *Everybody Comes to Rick's*.

14. Which film, released in the UK in 1941, became Charlie Chaplin's biggest box office hit?

15. In 1948, Laurence Olivier won the Academy Award for Best Actor for *Hamlet*. Two years earlier he was also nominated for which other Shakespearean film?

16. What is the name of Kane's vast palatial estate in *Citizen Kane*?

17. Edmund Gwenn won an Academy Award for Best Supporting Actor for which magical role in the 1947 classic *Miracle on 34th Street*?

18. In which Disney film, released in 1942, would you find a pink-nosed rabbit called Thumper and a skunk called Flower?

19. *Flying Tigers* was the first appearance in a war movie for one of the twentieth-century's biggest Hollywood stars. What was his name?

20. Who starred alongside Laurence Olivier as The Second Mrs de Winter in Alfred Hitchcock's psychological thriller *Rebecca*?

Saturday Afternoon Westerns

1. Which star of Western films was born Marion Mitchell Morrison?

2. Who played a lynching victim in the 1943 film *The Ox-Bow Incident* with Henry Fonda?

3. Which quiet-talking laconic hero of Westerns also appeared in the comedy films *My Favourite Wife* with Cary Grant and *Follow the Fleet* with Fred Astaire and Ginger Rogers?

4. Which actor starred as the unemployed cowhand Jim Garry in the 1948 black-and-white 'psychological' Western, *Blood on the Moon*?

5. Who was the male star of the 1947 film, *Angel and the Badman*?

6. The 1943 Howard Hughes film *The Outlaw* was the breakthrough role for which young actress and future Hollywood sex symbol?

7. Roy Rogers had a golden palomino called Trigger. What was the name of his German Shepherd dog?

8. *Virginia City* starred Randolph Scott, Errol Flynn and which other male screen legend?

9. Errol Flynn was the male lead of *They Died with Their Boots On.* Who was his female co-star?

10. Gene Autry had three famous Christmas hit songs: 'Here Comes Santa Claus', 'Frosty the Snowman' and which other?

11. Which musical cowboy was the first artist signed with Capitol Records and recorded the title-track song for High Noon, 'Do Not Forsake Me Oh My Darlin''?

12. Which Western star was one of the most decorated American soldiers of World War II?

13. On 12th October 1940, which 60-year-old cowboy of the silent era was killed by a suitcase when he crashed his yellow Cord Phaeton sports car into a gully?

14. The 1948 classic *Red River* starred John Wayne and which other moody, sensitive young method actor?

15. *My Darling Clementine* is a retelling of which notorious incident in the history of the American Wild West?

16. 'Happy Trails' was the theme song for which famous Western couple?

17. In 1940, the comedy Western *Go West* starred which family comedy act?

18. Who had a famous horse named Tony?

19. In 1940, who won his third Academy Award for Best Supporting Actor for his role as self-appointed hanging judge Roy Bean in *The Westerner* with Gary Cooper?

20. In 1946, Jennifer Jones, Joseph Cotten, Gregory Peck and Lillian Gish starred in the sexually-charged film *Duel in the Sun.* What was its racy nickname?

Famous Film Quotes

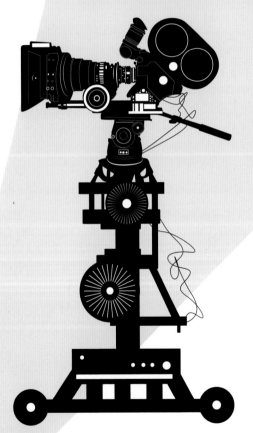

Who said it and in what film?

1. 'I'm sorry, but I don't want to be an emperor.'

2. 'You can't fool me. There ain't no Sanity Clause!'

3. 'Oh, Jerry, don't let's ask for the moon. We have the stars.'

4. 'We'll always have Paris.'

5. 'In Switzerland they had brotherly love – and 500 years of democracy and peace, and what did that produce? The cuckoo clock.'

6. 'It's Mrs Danvers. She's gone mad! She said she'd rather destroy Manderley than see us happy here.'

7. 'Made it, Ma! Top of the world!'

8. 'I can't believe it. Right here where we live – right here in St. Louis.'

9. 'Badges? We ain't got no badges! We don't need no badges! I don't have to show you any stinking badges!'

10. 'You know how to whistle, don't you, Steve? You just put your lips together and blow.'

11. 'This is the end! The absolute end!'

12. 'I haven't been afraid since I've known you.'

13. 'Put me in your pocket, Mike.'

14. 'Rosebud.'

15. 'My mother thanks you. My father thanks you. My sister thanks you. And I thank you.'

16. 'Insanity runs in my family. It practically gallops.'

17. 'Round up the usual suspects.'

18. 'Thank you for coming back to me.'

19. 'Clarence! Clarence! Help me, Clarence! Get me back! Get me back.'

20. 'What's wrong with you?' 'Nothing you can't fix.'

Fashion

1. What did Oliver Lyttleton, President of the Board of Trade, announce on 1st June, 1941 that was to have a direct impact on the British fashion industry?

2. Which British designer unveiled the first collection of Utility Dresses for women in 1942, and went on to design women's Army and Navy uniforms?

3. What wartime restriction to men's clothing saw men routinely order trousers that were too long in the leg?

4. Which two wartime restrictions necessitated the widespread use by men of braces?

5. In 1943, the Ministry of Information published a pamphlet designed to help British householders find ways to keep up appearances in spite of clothing rationing. What was it called?

6. By the summer of 1944, sales figures in the US revealed that the women of America were buying one particular item of clothing five times more than they had done in previous years. What was it?

7. What was the London department store, Selfridges' ingenious response to Blackout conditions?

8. Name the all-in-one garment, designed for men and women to wear in the event of a night-time

air raid and favoured by Prime Minister Winston Churchill?

9. What service was offered to women at leg make-up bars in department stores across the country?

10. Which ubiquitous wartime logo was commonly known as 'The Cheeses'?

11. What did Hollywood idol, Veronica Lake agree to do in order to preserve the safety of female factory workers across the US and the UK?

12. What iconic fashion piece did *Woman Magazine* fashion expert, Anne Edwards, demonstrate the construction of for women in a 1942 Pathé newsreel, using two scarves?

13. Whose first collection, released in 1947 and dubbed 'The New Look', rescued France's ailing fashion industry with cinched-in waists and full skirts?

14. When a key wartime industry announced a reversion to peacetime production in August 1945, women rioted outside department stores across America. What were they fighting for?

15. What fashion trend was known as the Victory Roll?

16. To whom did British Army servicemen commonly refer as the 'Brylcreem Boys'?

17. What was the brand name of a range of highly patriotic, decorated silk scarves designed by Arnold Lever in London?

18. What product did Helena Rubenstein name 'Regimental Red'?

19. The increasing shortage of what product saw an increase in the use of lemon juice, beer and vinegar?

20. What did a wartime Ministry of Supply memo rank as essential to the morale of women as tobacco was for men?

Frank Sinatra

1. His mother was a midwife; what two jobs did his illiterate father do?

2. How did he get the scar that ran from the left corner of his mouth to his jawline?

3. In 1939, he released his first commercial record. What was its title?

4. Shortly afterwards he spent four years as the lead singer with which trombone-playing big band leader?

5. His contract stated that he must pay 43 per cent commission on his earnings for the rest of his life; however, when he went solo he bought his way out for a few thousand dollars, leading many to speculate that he had used his connections with which organisation?

6. During his early career what smooth-sounding name did he refuse to adopt despite the insistence of his management?

FRANK SINATRA

7. Apart from 'Ol' Blue Eyes', what was Sinatra's other nickname?

8. In 1945, he made a short film that opposed anti-Semitism and racial intolerance. What was it called?

9. How did he escape being drafted into the army during the war?

10. Name his two co-stars in the 1945 musical film *Anchors Aweigh*?

11. In 1946, Sinatra's debut album, *The Voice of Frank Sinatra*, was an early example of what?

12. Sinatra was married four times. Nancy Barbato and Barbara Marx were wives number one and four. Who came in between?

13. Barbara Marx was the ex-wife of which Marx brother?

14. Name the show tune from the Rodgers and Hammerstein musical *Oklahoma!* that was a hit separately for Bing Crosby, Sinatra and The Ink Spots.

15. Sinatra released two different songs with the same name, the second of which became one of his signature hits in the late seventies. What was the title?

16. Sinatra worked frequently with which popular American close harmony singing group on the radio during the forties?

17. Sinatra always refused to perform in Las Vegas hotels and casinos if they practiced what policy?

18. Which 1949 musical film starred Sinatra as Chip, one of three sailors on shore leave in New York?

19. In 1949, his fourth album was panned by the critics. What was its title?

20. His career briefly nosedived during the early fifties and Sinatra attempted suicide after seeing girls in Times Square queuing excitedly for the next teen idol (who later married Elizabeth Taylor). What was his name?

ITMA

1. What does ITMA stand for?

2. ITMA began in 1939. Which year did it abruptly end and why?

3. What was New Zealander Ted Kavanagh's role in the show?

4. For which character is Dorothy Summers best remembered?

5. What was her catchphrase?

6. Who voiced the crapulent Colonel Chinstrap?

7. What was his catchphrase?

8. Who played the gluttonous Sophie Tuckshop?

9. What was her catchphrase?

10. What were the names of the two moving men voiced by Jack Train and Horace Percival?

11. What was their catchphrase?

12. What was the name of the old dithering character who always had to ask his dad?

13. Deryck Guyler claimed that his character, Frisby Dike, was the first person to be heard on the radio with which UK regional accent?

14. What was the name of the seedy fictional seaside resort of

which Handley became mayor?

15. From June 1941 the title was changed to reflect this new seaside location. What did it become?

16. What was the name of Handley's pier diving character?

17. He subsequently become Governor of which fictional South Sea island?

18. What was the name of the German spy?

19. What was his catchphrase?

20. What parting exclamation, subsequently made famous by Homer Simpson, was frequently used by the character Miss Hotchkiss?

The Forces' Sweethearts

Vera Lynn

1. What was Vera Lynn's maiden name?

2. She grew up in London's East End. What was her father's trade?

3. How old was she when she left school to become a full-time performer?

4. She made her first radio broadcast in 1935 with the same popular big band that later made Rose Brennan a star. What was its name?

5. She made her first commercial record with an American-born British musician whose signature tune was 'Clap Hands, Here Comes Charlie'. What was his name?

6. Her first solo record is a phrase that means going to bed. What was it?

7. She first sang 'We'll Meet Again' in 1939 while touring with which dance band?

8. In 1939 she married a clarinettist

in the band. What was his name?

9. What was the name of the morale-boosting BBC radio programme that Vera Lynn hosted for soldiers posted abroad?

10. Which Vera Lynn 'goodbye' song was the first by a British singer to top the charts in the United States?

11. Which Vera Lynn song first appeared in the 1939 Carroll Levis film *Discoveries*, sung by the boy soprano Glyn Davies?

12. She made three films during the forties: *Rhythm Serenade, One Exciting Night* and which other?

13. Her 1943 hit 'You'll Never Know' originally appeared in the film *Hello Frisco* sung by which American actress and singer?

14. According to the lyric, 'When the lights go on again all over the world . . . a kiss won't mean goodbye' but what?

15. After the war ended, Vera had a daughter. What was her name?

16. Which post-war song topped the UK charts in 1954 and was her only British No. 1?

17. In 1962, Vera Lynn appeared as herself in a Danish comedy war film directed by Annelise Reenberg. What was its title?

18. Which Vera Lynn classic is featured at the end of Stanley Kubrick's 1964 film *Dr Strangelove*?

19. How did she enter the record books in 2009 aged 92?

20. Why will there never be wild bluebirds over the White Cliffs of Dover?

Classic Forties Novels

Name the Classic Forties Novels in Which These Characters Appear

1. Jo, Bessie and Fanny

2. Nicholas Salmanovitch Rubashov

3. Robert Jordan

4. Meursault

5. Mayzie bird

6. Captain Charles Ryder

CLASSIC FORTIES NOVELS

7. Philip Rhayader

8. Joseph Knecht

9. Gulley Jimson

10. Winston Smith

11. Kino

12. Lord Sepulchrave

13. Geoffrey Firmin

14. Snowball

15. Port Moresby

16. Cassandra Mortmain

17. Peter, Susan, Edmund and Lucy Pevensie

18. Henry Scobie

19. General Edward Cummings, Sam Croft, Woodrow Wilson, Robert Hearn, Roy Gallagher

20. Brat Farrar

Nat King Cole

1. Name the capital city of the US state of Alabama where Nathaniel Adams Coles was born.

2. When he was four years old, he and his family moved to the Bronzeville neighbourhood of which vibrant blues city?

3. What was his father's profession?

4. How old was Cole when he married his first wife?

5. At the age of twenty, Cole started a jazz trio. Its unique signature sound developed because of the absence of which musical instrument, normally found in a band?

6. Name the jazz pianist who was one of Cole's greatest inspirations.

7. What was the original name of the King Cole Trio?

8. Cole's first mainstream vocal hit was his 1943 recording in which a buzzard takes different animals for a joyride. What was its title?

9. The King Cole Trio performed twice on a CBS Radio variety show hosted by Orson Welles. What was the show's title?

10. Song writing partners, Mel Torme and Bob Wells wrote 'The Christmas Song' on a blisteringly hot July day in California. How does it begin?

11. In Los Angeles on Sunday 2nd July 1944, Cole played jazz piano during the first of many iconic concerts staged and recorded by jazz music impresario Norman Granz under the acronym JATP. What does it stand for?

12. Name the love song that became Cole's first No. 1 pop single on 28th December, 1946 and repeats the phrase, 'I hope you do believe me' three times.

13. Which of his hits was re-recorded by several artists including Chuck Berry, The Rolling Stones and Depeche Mode?

14. Cole released 'Nature Boy' in March 1948. Complete its haunting last line: 'The greatest thing you'll ever learn is . . .'

15. Name Cole's 1951 million-selling hit that was later covered by both Donny Osmond and Michael Jackson.

16. Which hit was written for the film *Captain Carey, U.S.A.* with the enigmatic subject of a painting by Leonardo da Vinci?

17. Cole's signature tune was written by Irving Gordon and recorded in 1951 with the working title 'Uncomparable'. What was its finished title?

18. Completed in 1956, the new Capitol Records building near Hollywood and Vine in Los Angeles was nicknamed 'The House that Nat Built' because he had earned the company so much money. It was the first office building of its kind to be built in what shape?

19. In 1956, Cole became the first African-American performer to do what?

20. Name his famous daughter who was also a singer.

Opening Lines

Name That Tune

1. 'Now it's funny where some women live who sing upon the stage.'

2. 'That certain night, the night we met.'

3. 'Of all the boys I've known, and I've known some.'

4. 'I dreamed of two blue orchids.'

5. 'Come to the station, jump from the train.'

6. 'I've just got here, through Paris, from the sunny southern shore.'

7. 'And now the purple dusk of twilight time.'

8. 'He was a famous trumpet man from out Chicago way.'

9. 'Oh, give me land, lots of land under starry skies above.'

10. 'I don't know why but I'm feeling so sad.'

11. 'Oh the weather outside is frightful.'

12. 'Darling, I'm so blue without you.'

13. 'I wrote my mother, I wrote my father.'

14. 'For years we had an aspidistra in a flowerpot.'

15. 'A rose must remain with the sun and the rain.'

16. 'You had plenty money, 1922.'

17. 'East is east and west is west.'

18. 'Don't know why there's no sun up in the sky.'

19. 'There was a boy.'

20. 'There's just one place for me.'

Wireless Quiz

1. Which Sunday lunchtime radio programme regularly featured Alan Breeze, resident singer Kathie Kay and the pianist Russ Conway?

2. Which thriller serial popularised the catchphrase 'With one bound Dick was free'?

3. Which Sunday lunchtime radio show had the theme tune 'With A Song in My Heart' and was presented by Cliff Michelmore?

4. Which popular music show was introduced every morning by the theme tune 'In Party Mood' by Jack Strachey?

5. Name the *Merry-Go-Round* comedy show that starred Kenneth Horne and Richard Murdoch as thick-witted senior officers in a fictional RAF station?

6. *Merry-Go-Round* also included a naval show set in Sinking-in-the-Ooze. What was the name of the hapless ship?

7. What was the name of the *Merry-Go-Round* army show that starred comedian 'Cheerful' Charlie Chester?

8. Which sporting programme aired from 5.00 to 6.00 pm on Saturday evenings from 1948 and was originally presented by Raymond Glendenning?

9. The radio comedy *Take It From Here* ran from 1948 to 1960 and introduced the spin-off characters Ron and his long-term fiancée Eth. What was their lugubrious family name?

WIRELESS QUIZ

10. Which Sunday evening variety show was hosted by Philip Slessor and launched the career of Frankie Howerd?

11. Name the Welsh variety show that always closed with the song, 'We'll Keep a Welcome (in the Hillsides)'.

12. Which long-running programme debuted on 7th October, 1946 hosted by Alan Ivimey but has since enjoyed a succession of exclusively female presenters including Joan Griffiths, Violet Carson, Judith Chalmers and Jenni Murray?

13. *Band Waggon* was the first comedy show tailored specifically for the wireless. It starred Richard Murdoch, Syd Walker and which Liverpool-born catchphrase comic?

14. What was the name of their cleaning lady?

15. Which suburban serial drama popularised the phrase 'I'm rather worried about Jim'?

16. Which horror drama series opened with Valentine Dyall's ominous voiceover: 'This is your story-teller, The Man in Black'?

17. What was the name of Liverpudlian comic Ted Ray's long-running radio show that began in 1949?

18. Which future Doctor Who starred in the radio comedy *Up the Pole* with Variety comedians Jimmy Jewel and Ben Warriss?

19. Academy Award winning actress and singer Julia Elizabeth Wells appeared several times on *Up the Pole* when she was a child. By what name is she best known?

20. Which English comedian had his own radio show that ran for three series during 1944 and 1945 and is best remembered for playing inept schoolmasters?

The Sporting Forties

1. Japan forfeited hosting the 1940 Olympic Games to which North European city before its eventual cancellation?

2. On November 15, 1947, which cricketer became the first non-Englishman to achieve his hundredth first-class century?

3. In 1949, which baseball team beat the Brooklyn Dodgers four games to one to win the World Series?

4. The 1946–7 football season was the first league competition since the outbreak of World War II. Which team topped the First Division to win the title?

5. On 6th July, 1941, the New York Yankees unveiled a monument in centrefield to which recently deceased first baseman?

6. Nicknamed 'The Wardrobe' because of his flamboyant clothes, which American professional golfer won the Masters Tournament in 1940, 1947 and 1950?

7. In 1949, Ted Schroeder (USA) defeated Jaroslav Drobný (Czechoslovakia) to win which sporting championship?

8. Which two rugby teams shared victory at the 1947 Five Nations Championship?

9. In Game 3 of the 1947 World Series, who hit the first pinch-hit home run in World Series history?

10. In 1941, whose 56-game hitting streak was the longest in baseball history?

11. Which baseball legend died on 16th August, 1948?

12. On 2nd March 1940, which legendary thoroughbred racehorse won the $121,000 Santa Anita Handicap in his final race?

13. In July 1948, which Italian cyclist won three consecutive mountain stages in the Tour de France – a feat that has never been equalled?

14. Who retired in 1946 after winning his fifteenth consecutive World Snooker Championship?

15. Nicknamed the 'Brown Bomber', which boxing legend held the world heavyweight championship from 1937 to 1949?

16. On April 26, 1941, which musical instrument was used for the first time at a baseball stadium?

17. In 1940, which National Hunt steeplechase was won by Bogskar?

18. In 1946, the FA Cup was played for the first time since the outbreak of World War II. Which team beat Charlton Athletic 4–1 after extra time to claim the trophy?

19. In 1947, Jackie Robinson debuted for the Brooklyn Dodgers. Why was this significant?

20. Which team beat Blackpool 4–2 to win the 1948 FA Cup?

Thirty Forties Hits

Name the singers most associated with the song

1. 'Chattanoogie Shoe Shine Boy'

2. '(I've Got A Gal In) Kalamazoo'

3. 'Ac-Cent-Tchu-Ate The Positive'

4. 'Amapola'

5. 'As Time Goes By'

THIRTY FORTIES HITS

6. 'Auld Lang Syne'

7. 'Ballerina'

8. 'Boogie Woogie Bugle Boy'

9. '(I Love You)
   For Sentimental Reasons'

10. 'Der Fuehrer's Face'

11. 'G.I. Jive'

12. 'God Bless The Child'

13. 'I Don't Want To Set The World
    On Fire'

14. 'I'll Never Smile Again'

15. 'I'll Walk Alone'

16. 'I'm looking Over A Four Leaf
    Clover'

17. 'Jersey Bounce'

18. 'Jingle, Jangle, Jingle'

19. 'Manana (Is Soon Enough For
    Me)'

20. 'Maria Elena'

21. 'Maybe (you'll think of me
    when you are all alone)'

22. 'Mule Train'

23. 'Near You'

24. 'On the Atchison, Topeka
    and the Santa Fe'

25. 'Paper Doll'

26. 'Pistol Packin' Mama'

27. 'Praise The Lord And Pass
    The Ammunition!'

28. 'Rag Mop'

29. 'Riders In The Sky
    (A Cowboy Legend)'

30. 'Sentimental Journey'

Forties Hollywood Musical Lyrics:

Name the Song

1. 'Listen to my tale of woe,
   It's terribly sad, but true.'

2. 'They say some people long ago
   were searching for a different
   tune, one that they could croon.'

3. 'Ding dong, ding dong, do you
   hear the bells call ding dong?'

4. 'You'll feel blue, you'll feel
   sad, you'll miss the dearest
   pal you've ever had.'

FORTIES HOLLYWOOD MUSICAL LYRICS: NAME THE SONG

5. 'Dreams were never lovelier, pardon me if I stare.'

6. 'Where the treetops glisten and children listen to hear sleigh bells in the snow.'

7. 'A real life nephew of my Uncle Sam, born on the fourth of July.'

8. 'The sun is bringing a new day tomorrow.'

9. 'Let your heart be light, From now on our troubles will be out of sight.'

10. 'A mule is an animal with long funny ears, Kicks up at anything he hears.'

11. 'So here's to the beautiful ladies, here's to those wonderful girls.'

12. 'Every time you're near a rose, Aren't you glad you've got a nose?'

13. 'Put 'em all together they spell Susie, the sweetheart of the boys at sea.'

14. 'Never saw the sun, shining so bright, never saw things going so right.'

15. 'Starlight and dew drops are waiting for thee.'

16. 'Act the fool, play the calf, And you'll always have the last laugh.'

17. 'I could hardly wait, to keep our date this lovely Easter morning.'

18. 'Gotta see the whole town right from Yonkers on down to the Bay, in just one day.'

19. 'Nelly Kelly loved baseball games, knew the players, knew all their names.'

20. 'The way you wear your hat, The way you sip your tea.'

The Forces' Sweethearts

Jane Russell

1. What was her original Christian name: Bernado, Roberto or Ernestine?

2. Her father was a US Army lieutenant. What did her mother do?

3. She was discovered by Howard Hughes working as an assistant to his: dentist, chiropodist or chiropractor?

4. For her 1943 debut film, what did director Howard Hughes invent and design specially for her to accentuate her assets?

5. The film also starred Jack Buetel as which real-life American Old West gunfighter?

6. Why did Howard Hughes try to get the film banned?

80

7. The iconic publicity shot for the film showed her lying on a pile of what?

8. In the photo she had one hand behind her head. What did she hold in the other hand?

9. Why was the film quickly banned upon its initial release?

10. Which comedian and co-star once introduced her as 'the two and only Miss Russell'?

11. In what year was the ban lifted after Hughes had made extensive cuts?

12. In her next film she played journalist Joan Kenwood, mourning the death of her Air Corps photographer husband during WWII. What was its title?

13. Name the 1948 spoof western in which she starred with Bob Hope.

14. Her character in this film was based on which real-life American frontierswoman and professional scout?

15. Name the 1953 film in which she and Marilyn Monroe played American showgirls.

16. Name the song from the film in which Monroe sang while wearing an iconic pink dress, surrounded by well-dressed suitors.

17. Monroe's salary for the film was $15,000. How much did Jane Russell receive: $15,000, $50,000 or $400,000?

18. Name her two co-stars in the 1951 film *Double Dynamite*: one played a bank teller suspected of embezzlement, the other was a wisecracking waiter.

19. Which cleft-chinned tough guy played the professional gambler Dan Milner in her 1951 film noir, *His Kind of Woman*?

20. True or false: a pair of mountains in Alaska are officially named 'The Jane Russell Peaks' in her honour.

Bob Hope

1. What was his birth name: Leslie Townes Hope, Terry Gordon Hope or Kenneth Budd Hope?

2. His parents emigrated to the US when he was five years old. In which city was he born?

3. His father was a stonemason in which English seaside resort in North Somerset?

4. In 1915, aged 12, he won an amateur talent competition for his impersonation of which English comic actor and filmmaker?

5. Name the corpulent scandal-ridden silent film actor who gave him his first job in show business by finding him work in a small touring troupe.

6. He changed his name to Bob in 1929, reputedly after the American racing driver who set the world speed record of 140.21 mph in Daytona Beach, Florida on 23rd April, 1911. What was his name?

7. Name the song of gratitude from the film *The Big Broadcast of 1938* that is considered to be his signature tune.

8. Which contact sport did he briefly pursue professionally under the pseudonym 'Packy East'?

9. Name his female co-star in the 1947 American romantic comedy film *My Favourite Brunette*.

10. What style of film did *My Favourite Brunette* parody?

11. Between 1941 and 1978, what ceremony did he host more than any other performer?

12. Which former US President was a close friend for 40 years until his death in April 1994?

13. Name the entertainer and close friend with whom he maintained a long-running public comic feud?

14. Name the 28-year-old starlet who replaced Dorothy Lamour in the final *Road to…* film.

15. True or False: He starred in the film *Some Like It Hot*?

16. Paulette Goddard starred with Bob Hope in the films *The Ghost Breakers* (1940) and *Nothing but the Truth* (1941). Who was her estranged film star husband at the time?

17. In 1983, he was inducted into which sporting Hall of Fame?

18. He was married to his second wife for 69 years, but conducted many affairs. Which one of his mistresses was jokingly referred to in Hollywood circles as 'Mrs Bob Hope'?

19. Which iconic American comic actress starred with him in the films *Sorrowful Jones* and *Fancy Pants*.

20. In 1998, what did Queen Elizabeth II award him?

Cary Grant

1. Born Archibald Alexander Leach in 1904, he spent his unhappy early childhood in a suburb of which British city?

2. Who was the German-American female star of the 1932 film, *Blonde Venus* in which he appeared?

3. Which comic actress delivered the now famous line 'Why don't you come up sometime and see me?' in another early Grant film, *She Done Him Wrong*?

4. Who was his leading lady in the films *Holiday, Sylvia Scarlett, Bringing Up Baby* and *The Philadelphia Story*?

5. In the 1938 screwball comedy, *Bringing Up Baby*, what kind of animal was 'Baby'?

6. Grant plays a mild-mannered palaeontologist who is one 'intercostal clavicle' short of assembling the entire skeleton of what?

7. Name the 1940 romantic comedy film that starred Cary Grant, Katharine Hepburn and James Stewart, based on a Broadway play of the same name.

8. What proportion of his fee for making this film did he donate to British War Relief Society?

9. Name the 1941 Hitchcock romantic psychological thriller that starred Cary Grant and Joan Fontaine as a married couple.

10. In this film Grant brings his wife a drink that she believes has been poisoned. What was the drink?

11. In 1942, Grant and his second wife were nicknamed 'Cash and Cary' because she was one of the richest heiresses in the world. What was her name?

12. Name Frank Capra's 1944 dark comedy in which Mortimer Brewster (Grant) discovers that his two dotty aunts have been poisoning men and burying them in the cellar.

13. His 1944 film, *None but the Lonely Heart*, is named after a well-known song that was used as background music, written by which late-Romantic Russian composer?

14. In the 1946 biopic *Night and Day*, Grant played which American composer and songwriter?

15. Which 17-year-old former child star became infatuated with sophisticated bachelor Richard Nugent (Grant) in the 1947 film *The Bachelor and the Bobby-Soxer*?

16. Name the 1946 Hitchcock post-war psychological thriller starring Cary Grant, Ingrid Bergman and Claude Rains.

17. One of the film's most famous cinematic moments begins with a wide shot above a sweeping staircase that slowly closes in on Ingrid Bergman's left hand. What is she holding?

18. Name the film in which Grant appeared with Ginger Rogers, Charles Coburn and Marilyn Monroe that shares its simian title with a 1931 Marx Brothers comedy.

19. Late in her career his fourth ex-wife played Judge Jennifer 'Whipper' Cone in the American legal comedy-drama series, *Ally McBeal*. What was her name?

20. Which film director – who used Grant in four of his films – described him as 'the only actor I ever loved in my whole life'?

The Forces' Sweethearts

Judy Garland

1. She was born on 10th June, 1922 as: Frances Ethel Gumm, June Gladys Garfield or Jessica Jane Bunting?

2. She changed her performing name to Judy after a song by which Award-winning singer-songwriter of 'Stardust', 'Ole Buttermilk Sky' and 'Georgia on My Mind'?

3. At the 1940 Academy Awards ceremony, she received an Academy Juvenile Award for her performances including *Babes in Arms* (1939) and which other film released that year?

4. Who did MGM studio chief, Louis B. Mayer, try to cast in the role of Dorothy in *The Wizard of Oz* before Judy?

5. Successive critical Hollywood producers damaged her self-esteem throughout her career. What did Louis B. Mayer call her?

6. Which former child star played the title role in her 1940 film *Andy Hardy Meets Debutante*?

7. What type of scene did Judy perform in the musical comedy film *Little Nellie Kelly* for the first and only time in her career?

8. The same film was also famous for showing her first what with her co-star, George Murphy?

9. With which bandleader did she have an affair before he eloped with Lana Turner?

10. Who made his film debut as her male co-star in the 1942 musical film, *For Me and My Gal*?

11. Name the 1943 film in which she was given the full Hollywood glamour treatment to make her screen transition from girl-next-door to adult glamour puss?

12. In which film did she sing, 'Have Yourself a Merry Little Christmas'?

13. Judy gave birth to a daughter on 12th March, 1946. What was her name?

14. During the mid-forties, with which legendary film director did she conduct a brief affair while he was married to Rita Hayworth?

15. Why did her 1945 film *The Clock* disappoint many moviegoers?

16. *The Clock* was directed by her future husband. What was his name?

17. How many times did she marry?

18. In 1948, she scored her top grossing hit film with Fred Astaire and Peter Lawford. It included the songs, 'Steppin' Out With My Baby' and 'Easter Parade'. What was its title?

19. She was immediately reunited with Astaire in *The Barkleys of Broadway*, but ill health forced her replacement by which of his former leading ladies?

20. Name her final MGM film in which she first sang 'Get Happy'.

The Home Guard

1. On 14th May 1940, Secretary of State for War, Anthony Eden, made a radio announcement calling on men over the age of 17 to enrol in the LDV. What did the acronym – the original name of the Home Guard – stand for?

2. What was the upper age limit?

3. Arming and clothing the LDV was a continual challenge. Why did one million armbands make Eden reluctant to rename the force?

4. Why did disgruntled LDV members break into museums?

5. Approximately how many men were eventually recruited into the Home Guard: 750,000, 1.7 million or 2.5 million?

6. What was the Amazon Defence Corps and why did it form?

7. True or false: The Home Guard never fired a single shot in anger during WWII?

8. What medal was awarded to anyone serving in the Home Guard for more than three years?

9. Why did many volunteers have Webley Mk VI .455 revolvers?

10. In 1942, Churchill ordered 250,000 pikes to arm the Home Guard. Why were these ineffectual weapons disparagingly christened 'Croft's Pikes'?

11. What did the codeword 'Cromwell' indicate?

12. What did the codeword 'Oliver' indicate?

13. Why was the ringing of church bells strictly controlled?

14. Fill in the missing word from Anthony Eden's speech to the House of Commons in November 1940: 'No one will claim for the Home Guard that it is a miracle of organisation ... but many would claim that it is a miracle of _____.'

15. Who wrote the 1943 song, 'Could You Please Oblige Us With a Bren Gun?' that ridiculed the chronic lack of supplies within the force?

16. Name Michael Powell and Emeric Pressburger's 1943 film about a retired Colonel who joins the Home Guard.

17. In the 1943 comedy film *Get Cracking*, which Lancashire-born comedian starred with Dinah Sheridan as a Home Guard lance corporal who builds a homemade tank?

18. How many members of the Home Guard were posthumously awarded the George Cross: none, two or eight?

19. Name the comedian whose monologue character Sam Small managed to join the Home Guard, despite being a veteran of the Battle of Waterloo.

20. Name the fictional south coast town that was the setting for the television comedy series *Dad's Army*.

Household Products

Advertising Slogans

Which household products were advertised using these slogans?

1. If it's chocolate then it's FOOD.

2. Sustaining! because made with chocolate. Energising! because it includes Glucose. Nourishing! because it contains milk.

3. The more you work, the better sleep you need.

ADVERTISING SLOGANS – HOUSEHOLD PRODUCTS

4. Remember Jones, the army marches on its stomach!

5. Get whites whiter without bleaching!

6. Sets a new standard of whiteness and brightness.

7. Swish and the grease is gone, now I've gone modern with _____.

8. By _____! that's quick!

9. Look! Your smooth hands show you _____ is the mildest household soap.

10. It's Proctor & Gamble's miracle! Oceans of suds! No water softeners needed!

11. _____: the backbone of young Britain.

12. How dull winter meals could be . . . but for Benedict _____. They're the making of the meal.

13. Spread Extra Goodness – with _____ at Tea-time.

14. The lucky dog! That's Baby's precious _____.

15. Don't forget the _____. It adds the appetising flavour of Beef.

16. Delicious-NEW! Birds Eye Quick-Frozen _____! Just heat and serve!

17. _____ makes milk go further!

18. You can depend on it. It's extra Vitamin B you need. _____ Brown Bread.

19. When he's back to the meals that mother makes. Ah! _____

20. _____ are particularly good. They are made by particular people for particular people.

Advertising Slogans II

Which household products were advertised using these slogans?

1. Insist on _____ and you'll get it.

2. Mummy says _____ & _____ – nothing else will do.

3. Get it! Cook it! Taste It! The satisfying pudding with the famous flavour.

4. Soon you'll have _____! Fancy calling _____ margarine!

5. I start the day with a 30-second breakfast.

6. If you don't sleep well at night take ENO's _____ first thing every morning.

ADVERTISING SLOGANS II – HOUSEHOLD PRODUCTS

7. Goodness! Your baker bakes it.

8. Come to where the flavour is.
   Come to _____ Country.

9. _____ puts a
   smile into vegetables.

10. Wake up gay in the
    morning! _____.
    The world's best nightcap.

11. She's engaged! She's lovely!
    She uses _____!

12. Behind the workers. Behind
    the men. Behind the guns.
    _____ tablets.

13. Skin needs _____. Doctors
    use and recommend it.

14. It's wonderful to be in love!
    How foolish to miss your
    chance through dry, lifeless
    'middle-age' skin! _____
    Made with olive oil!

15. They cheer one up just to
    look at them, Mr Barratt!
    Walk the Barratt way.

16. Bath-time sweetness all day
    long. _____ checks
    perspiration instantly. Gives
    1 to 3 days' protection.

17. Packed with pleasure.
    _____ Please.

18. New improved _____
    shampoo now gives your hair
    a sensational new shine!

19. My dear! This coffee is
    marvellous! How on earth
    did you make it so quickly?
    _____: made in an
    instant – right in the cup!

20. Laugh it off with _____!

Winston Churchill

1. Churchill was born on 30th November 1874, two months prematurely, in which palace in Oxfordshire?

2. At which top public school was he educated?

3. After a lacklustre school career, which college did he eventually join in 1893 after twice failing the entrance exam?

4. Which regiment did he join?

5. How did he first come to the attention of the public after graduation?

6. In 1895, he reported on the Cuban War of Independence during which he was awarded a medal and developed a lifelong love of which trademark luxury?

7. At what sport did the young cavalryman excel in his regiment?

8. He left the army in 1889 but initially failed to win a by-election in which constituency?

9. He subsequently reported on the Boer War, where his bravery during an ambush could have won him the Victoria Cross. Why was he ineligible?

10. He finally became an MP in 1900 and wrote an acclaimed two-volume biography of which politician and former Chancellor of the Exchequer?

11. In 1904, he crossed the floor to sit as a member of which political party?

12. Who did he marry on 12th September, 1908?

13. He helped to draft the Mental Deficiency Act 1913. What did he propose should happen to the 'feeble minded'?

14. Which office did he hold during the First World War and again in September 1939, on the day Britain declared war on Germany?

15. What additional military role did he create for himself, making him the most powerful Prime Minister in British history?

16. How old was he when he became Prime Minister?

17. In his first speech as PM he famously declared 'I have nothing to offer but blood, toil, —— and ——'.

18. Churchill warned: 'This is not the end. It is not even the beginning of the end. But it is, perhaps, the end of the beginning' after which Allied victory?

19. What did he win in 1953 'for his mastery of historical and biographical description'?

20. Two years before his death he became the first person to receive what US honour?

The Home Front

1. What were issued to civilians on 26th September, 1938?

2. Who were known as 'Ninos'?

3. What was imposed on the British population on 1st September 1939, two days before the outbreak of war?

4. In the early days of the war, what killed more British civilians than enemy action?

5. What was the name of the jingle that was designed to increase safety during blackouts?

6. What did Ministry of Information posters urge people to wear to make them more visible to pedestrians and drivers during blackouts?

7. What speed limit was imposed on the roads during a blackout?

8. How much did an Anderson shelter cost?

9. How many people was it designed to accommodate?

10. What do the initials ARP stand for?

11. Where would you find a Morrison shelter?

12. What safety warning might you have seen painted on the pavement during the war?

13. The government produced a special child-friendly gas mask, using which two bright colours?

14. It was called the Mickey Mouse gas mask, even though it didn't resemble the Disney character. Why?

15. What rude noise could you make by blowing through the rubber of the gas mask?

16. During the war, nearly 80 per cent of boys and 70 per cent of girls between the ages of 14 and 17 were in what?

17. Captain W.E. Johns' novels about Biggles were hugely popular; what was the name of his female heroine?

18. Which English comedian referred to the American GIs as 'overpaid, oversexed and over here'?

19. What advice did the public information film *Miss Grant Goes to the Door* give?

20. At the end of the war, demobilised men were given a full set of clothes. What was it called?

You Lucky People

Tommy Trinder

1. Complete his opening catchphrase: 'The name's Trinder. That's T-R-I-N-D-E-R, pronounced _____'.

2. His first film featured the songs 'Save a Little Sunshine' and 'Nothing Can Worry Me Now'. What was its title?

3. Who co-starred with Trinder in the 1939 comedy *She Couldn't Say No* and also appeared in 'The Haunted Mirror' sequence of the horror film *Dead of Night*?

4. Name the 1940 comedy film in which Trinder played one of three drunken sailors who captured a German ship.

5. What was its similarly titled loose sequel, released in 1944, in which Trinder was transported back to Ancient Rome after being struck by lightening at Stonehenge?

6. In the 1940 musical comedy *Laugh It Off*, how did Trinder's character earn a commission?

7. Which bandleader also appeared in the film with his 'Gaucho Tango Orchestra?

8. In 1941, he made a MOI film called *Communal Kitchen: Eating Out With Tommy Trinder*. What did it promote?

YOU LUCKY PEOPLE – TOMMY TRINDER

9. In *The Foreman Went to France*, Trinder played an army driver in charge of a group of French refugee children. Which Scottish actor – who later found fame in *Upstairs, Downstairs* – debuted as Alastair 'Jock' MacFarlan, 19th Fusillers?

10. In the 1943 film, *The Bells Go Down*, Trinder played Tommy Turk, a gambler who joins the AFS. What was the AFS?

11. Which future *Doctor Who* actor played Brooks in the film?

12. Name the documentary style film that was released at the same time as *The Bells Go Down* but used real firefighters and footage from actual fires during the Blitz?

13. In the 1944 film *Champagne Charlie*, who played Trinder's musical hall rival, 'The Great Vance'?

14. Who played Bessie Bellwood in the film and is also best remembered for the 1949 Ealing Comedy, *Passport to Pimlico*?

15. In which film was Trinder's character killed by a collapsing chimney stack?

16. He was a lifelong supporter of which London football club?

17. True or false: In 1955, Trinder starred in a film called *You Lucky People*.

18. Which country in the Southern Hemisphere was the setting for his 1950 film, *Bitter Springs* that co-starred Chips Rafferty?

19. He is credited with a bar trick called 'Trinder's Impossibility' that required what item of currency?

20. In 1955, he became the first host on ITV's brand new West End variety show (and was succeeded by Bruce Forsyth in 1958). What was it called?

Ealing Comedies

1. *Hue and Cry* (1947) starred a Scottish actor who is best remembered for the 1954 film *The Belles of St Trinian's* in which he played Headmistress Millicent Fritton and her twin brother Clarence Fritton. What was his name?

2. T.E.B. Clarke wrote the screenplay for the film and later won the Academy Award for Best Original Screenplay for which Ealing crime caper?

3. Which American actress appeared in *Another Shore* and became a leading figure in British theatre?

4. Name the home town of the two Welsh coal miners in the BAFTA-nominated *A Run for Your Money*.

5. The pair win a trip to watch a rugby match at Twickenham. Who played the gardening columnist, Whimple, who was supposed to meet them at Paddington station?

6. Donald Houston played one of the Welshmen. In the same year he enjoyed another breakthrough role in *The Blue Lagoon* with the actress who had just starred as Ophelia in Laurence Olivier's film *Hamlet*. What was her name?

7. The other Welshman was played by an actor who later appeared as the murderous butler in the cult television series *Randall and Hopkirk (Deceased)*. What was his name?

8. Which actress played Mrs Pargiter in the film and was later associated with the catchphrase 'George, don't do that'?

9. Leslie Perrins also appeared in the film. What kind of roles did he usually play?

10. Who famously played eight characters in the 1949 black comedy, *Kind Hearts and Coronets*?

11. The title refers to a line in the poem, *Lady Clara Vere de Vere*, by which nineteenth-century Poet Laureate?

12. Name the husky-voiced siren who played Price's suburban mistress, Sibella.

13. Which Ealing film poster used the strap line: 'She loved a man; he loved an island': *Another Shore* or *A Run for Your Money*?

14. Who starred in the 1949 comedy *Passport to Pimlico* with Stanley Holloway, Hermione Baddeley and Barbara Murray and also played Madame Arcati in David Lean's film *Blithe Spirit*?

15. How do the residents of a street in Pimlico try to end rationing?

16. Two years earlier, Hermione Baddeley was praised for the film *Brighton Rock*. Who starred in his breakthrough role as the teenaged hoodlum, Pinkie Brown?

17. Charles Crichton directed several Ealing Comedies but he scored a huge international hit in his late seventies when he directed John Cleese and Michael Palin in which film?

18. Rarotonga features in *Another Shore*. What is it?

19. The 1949 comedy *Whisky Galore!* is based on the novel of the same name by which Scottish author?

20. Who played Captain Waggett, the uncompromising commanding officer of the local Home Guard?

Arthur Askey

1. English comedian Arthur Askey was known for his catchphrases, including 'Before your very eyes'. How did he commonly greet his audiences?

2. Where did Askey grow up?

3. Which song, first recorded in 1938, formed an integral part of his stage act throughout his career?

4. Which British radio comedy programme, which aired regularly until 1940, made Askey a household name?

5. Arthur Askey and his comedy partner Richard Murdoch re-wrote the series so that listeners were led to believe the pair shared an apartment at the top of which iconic building?

6. By which nickname was his partner, Richard Murdoch, commonly known?

7. Which film in 1940 catapulted Askey from radio comedy star to film star in the UK?

8. Which song, taken from the same film, was to become Arthur's theme tune?

9. In which 1940 film did Askey star as an Oxford undergraduate, with a plot (and title) that took inspiration from a late-Victorian stage play?

10. In 1941, Askey intended to record a song named after a prominent Nazi, who fled to Scotland on 10th May 1941, but it was banned by the War Office. Who was the subject of the song?

11. Which 1941 film saw Askey and his fellow travellers stranded overnight at a remote, haunted location?

12. In which 1942 film did Askey play a disgraced lowly employee at the BBC who is sent to a remote island filled with shipwrecked models, where he uncovers a Nazi plot?

13. In 1942, Askey recorded a song in honour of the Munitions Girls, who assembled munitions on the factory production lines. What was it called?

14. Which much-loved British female comedy and music-hall star also popularised the same song?

15. In which 1942 movie did Arthur join the army and fantasise about a legendary English monarch?

16. In which 1944 movie did he star opposite singer, Anne Shelton?

17. What common Ministry of Information wartime slogan featured in the movie?

18. What was the name of Askey's first television series, which aired after WWII?

19. Which music producer now owns the rights to all Askey movies?

20. What did Askey once describe as 'like breathing in and out – it's no effort at all'?

The Forces' Sweethearts

Gracie Fields

1. She was born over a fish and chip shop in which market town in Greater Manchester, Lancashire?

2. What was her birth name?

3. Which comedian and impresario did she meet in her teens and subsequently marry?

4. Who was the 'pride of our alley'?

5. Her signature song featured in her first film. What was its title?

6. Fields first worked with this comedian and monologist on her film *Sing As We Go* and afterwards they remained close friends. What was his name?

7. According to her popular song, where did she keep, 'one bridal gown, one eiderdown . . . ribbons and me bows . . . these and them and those'?

8. According to her popular song, what did she keep for years in a flower pot 'on the whatnot, near the 'atstand in the 'all'?

9. In her song 'Walter, Walter' what does she beg Walter to do?

10. Her 1939 film *Shipyard Sally* features which hit wartime parting song?

11. In 1940, she married the Italian silent comedy actor Monty Banks. Why did they leave the UK and settle in Santa Monica, California?

12. 'Sing As We Go' was later parodied by Monty Python in which song?

13. In one of her Christmas songs, which oversized instrument did she take to a party?

14. In which film did she play an Englishwoman trapped in Paris by the invasion of the Nazis?

15. In 1943, Katharine Hepburn, Ethel Merman, Tallulah Bankhead, Gypsy Rose Lee and Gracie Fields made cameo appearances in a film that took its name from which real-life New York City restaurant and nightclub for American and Allied servicemen?

16. Based on the novel *Buried Alive* by Arnold Bennett, in which 1943 comedy film did she star with Monty Woolley?

17. She teamed up with Woolley again, playing struggling vaudeville actress Molly Barry in this 1945 American comedy film set in pre-war London.

18. She visited 12 towns in a BBC radio show in 1947. What was its industrious title?

19. What national exhibition did she open in 1951?

20. On Boxing Day, 1960, she appeared in a half-hour show for the BBC with just her, a piano and an audience. What was the title of the show?

Max Miller

1. By what nickname was Miller commonly known?

2. In which seaside resort was Miller born and lived all his life?

3. Which 1940 film included a scene in which Miller, playing a comedian, performed his own variety stage act?

4. Which comic song, partly written by Miller in 1936, became his signature tune?

5. Complete the lyric: 'I fell in love with Mary from the Dairy, but Mary . . . '

6. In 1940, Miller co-starred in the wartime review, *Apple Sauce*, with which Forces' Sweetheart?

7. Miller starred in a 1940 film as 'Alexander the Greatest'. It is one of 75 lost or missing films labelled 'Most Wanted' by the British Film Institute. What was the title?

8. What was the name of Miller's final film, released in 1942?

9. By 1943, after three years of touring on the variety circuit, Miller had established himself as the country's leading stand-up comedian of his

generation and had earned himself what accolade?

10. Miller famously said that comedy was the one job you can do badly and no one will what?

11. Complete the catchphrase: 'It's people like you who . . . '

12. Many of Miller's jokes were prohibited from being broadcast. For what reason?

13. Commonly, on stage Miller would remove two items from his pocket, one coloured white and one blue, and ask the audience which one they'd rather him use. What were they?

14. To circumvent censorship restrictions, Miller often worked a particular technique into his act. What was it?

15. Which British comic star of the 1950s paid tribute to Miller by adopting his first name?

16. Complete the catchphrase: 'There'll never be . . . '

17. Miller was renowned in theatrical circles for never buying anyone a drink, and yet conversely made a private habit of what?

18. Which half of a world-famous US double act of the era said of Miller; 'His timing was perfect; he projected his personality as well, if not better, than any performer I have seen on either side of the Atlantic'.

19. Complete the joke: 'My wife's the ugliest woman in the world - I'd sooner take her with me on tour, than . . .'

20. According to his biographer, John East, Miller was once banned by the BBC for five years after an incident that took place during a live transmission. What happened?

Laurence Olivier

1. In 1930, his big West End break came when Noël Coward cast him as Victor Prynne in his new comedy of manners about a divorced couple. What was its title?

2. Coward became his mentor. What did Olivier claim that he had never done before meeting him?

3. At the beginning of his Hollywood career, which Hollywood legend fired him as her leading man in the 1933 film *Queen Christina* and replaced him with her ex-boyfriend, John Gilbert?

4. In 1935, John Gielgud and Laurence Olivier alternated the roles of Romeo and Mercutio in a celebrated production of *Romeo and Juliet*. Who played Juliet?

5. After becoming a film star during the thirties and joining The Old Vic theatre company, he divorced his first wife and married which Hollywood actress in August, 1940?

6. The same year the couple lost nearly all their life savings when a joint Shakespearean venture flopped on Broadway. Which play nearly bankrupted them?

7. In 1940, he received his second Academy Award nomination for which Alfred Hitchcock film?

8. To help the war effort, Alexander Korda directed him in *That Hamilton Woman*, playing which historical British Admiral?

9. In 1944, he directed and played the title role in the film version of which Shakespeare play?

10. Four years later, he directed and starred in the first British film to win the Academy Award for Best Picture and he won Best Actor. What was its title?

11. Which young actor appeared in the film as a spear carrier with no lines and later found fame as Count Dracula in a sequence of Hammer Horror films and in *The Lord of the Rings* film trilogy (2001–2003)?

12. During this era, Olivier formed a triumvirate that dominated the British stage with which other two actors?

13. During the first three seasons at The Old Vic, who played Uncle Vanya, Falstaff and took the title role in *Cyrano de Bergerac*?

14. How old was Olivier when he directed himself in *King Lear* at The Old Vic in 1946?

15. Who played The Fool?

16. How old was he when he attempted Lear again – this time on television?

17. Who played The Fool in that production?

18. In 1949, Olivier directed the English premiere of *A Streetcar Named Desire*. Who played the role of Blanche DuBois?

19. In which year did he receive a knighthood?

20. Which John Osborne play injected new life into Olivier's stage career during the late fifties?

Laurel and Hardy

1. By 1940, the American comedy duo Laurel and Hardy had already established themselves in an array of slapstick comedy movies. What was their signature tune?

2. Where was each of the men born?

3. Whenever Stan Laurel portrayed shock in a movie, what would he characteristically do while crying?

4. Stan Laurel's trademark flat-footed walk was achieved in part thanks to what costume adaptation?

5. What name did Laurel give to the pair's surreal comedy style (for instance, the scenes where Laurel would create a pipe with his own fist, add tobacco, light it and smoke from it nonchalantly)?

6. What was Oliver Hardy's trademark action involving his necktie, used to show his embarrassment?

7. In which 1940 film did Laurel play a character other than Stanley for the only time since first pairing up with Hardy in 1927?

8. Which was the last Laurel and Hardy movie to have been made under the guidance of producer Hal Roach in 1940?

9. In 1941, the pair made *Great Guns*, their first movie with Twentieth Century Fox. What did Fox not permit them to do for the first time in their careers together?

10. Which 1943 wartime movie ran with the tagline, 'Their gayest film glorifies our home front heroes'?

11. Which 1943 movie was named after a popular dance of the day?

12. In the same movie, the pair appears wearing Zoot Suits, for which the production team had to seek special dispensation. Why?

13. Which dimpled young actor, who would come to be known for his starring role in movies such as *The Night of the Hunter*, had a bit part in Laurel and Hardy's 1943 movie, *The Dancing Masters*?

14. In their 1944 movie, *The Big Noise*, the duo cut the amount of slapstick scenes in which they inflicted destruction. For what reason?

15. Complete the classic Stan Laurel joke: 'If you must make a noise, make it . . . '

16. Which *Simpsons* catchphrase has its origins in Laurel and Hardy's nemesis, James Finlayson?

17. Which British actor and comedian, known for his iconic physical comedy, once described Laurel and Hardy as, 'wonderfully, wonderfully funny'?

18. Complete the catchphrase: 'Well, here's another . . . '

19. Which modern Black Country comedian admitted to subjecting girlfriends to 'the Laurel and Hardy test': If she didn't laugh at the dance sequence from *Way Out West*, he 'wrote her off'?

20. What was Oliver Hardy's catchphrase, used when he was feeling most frustrated by Laurel's antics?

Overheard in the NAAFI

WWII Songs

1. 'Göring has only got one _____
Hitler's [are] so very _____

_____ so very similar
And _____ has no balls
at all.'

2. 'We're going to hang out the
washing on the _____
Have you any _____,
mother dear?'

3. 'Praise the Lord and pass the
_____.'

4. 'We'll gather lilacs in the spring
again.
And walk together down
_____.'

5. 'Kiss me goodnight, _____
Tuck me in my little _____.'

OVERHEARD IN THE NAAFI – WWII SONGS

6. 'I don't want to join the army, I don't want to _____.
I'd rather hang around _____.'

7. 'Oh I haven't seen old Hitler for _____.'

8. 'We're the D-Day dodgers out in _____.
Always on the vino, always on the _____.'

9. 'We are _____ army,
The ragtime infantry'

10. 'There'll always be _____.
While there's a country lane.'

11. 'Oh, shine on, shine on _____.'

12. 'Now imagine me in the Maginot Line
Sitting on a _____ in the Maginot Line.'

13. 'When der fuehrer says we is de master race
We heil heil right in _____,'

14. 'Well I did what I could with my _____.'

15. 'I heard your feet
But could not meet
My _____.'

Answers

The Year That Was – 1940

1. River Thames
2. It was the first German plane shot down over England.
3. RMS Queen Elizabeth
4. Metal security threads
5. Neville Chamberlain
6. Queen Wilhelmina of the Netherlands
7. British Commandos
8. Italy
9. Paris
10. RMS Lancastria
11. Music While You Work
12. The Battle of Britain
13. Leon Trotsky
14. London
15. Palaeolithic cave paintings
16. The George Cross
17. John Lennon
18. Balham
19. Coventry
20. St Paul's Cathedral

The Year That Was – 1941

1. Graham Chapman
2. Tobruk
3. Swansea
4. Provide supplies and munitions to allied nations
5. Greece
6. It captured a German U-110 submarine with the equipment on-board.
7. Rudolf Hess
8. HMS Hood
9. Bismarck
10. The Soviet Union
11. 'L' Detachment, Special Air Service Brigade (SAS)
12. Douglas Bader
13. Josef Jakobs
14. Leningrad
15. The Pentagon
16. Dumbo
17. HMS Ark Royal
18. Finland
19. Hawaii
20. Address a Joint session of the U.S. Congress

The Year That Was – 1942

1. The Mildenhall Treasure
2. Stephen Hawking
3. Helicopter
4. Carole Lombard
5. Vic Oliver
6. Princess Elizabeth (now Queen Elizabeth II)
7. Thailand
8. 'White Christmas'
9. Malta
10. Archbishop of Canterbury
11. Sobibór and Treblinka II
12. Mexico
13. Amsterdam
14. Oxfam
15. Bambi
16. Waterloo Bridge
17. Prince George, Duke of Kent, brother of George VI
18. RMS Queen Mary
19. Milk
20. The Beveridge Report

The Year That Was – 1943

1. Casablanca
2. The Pentagon
3. Battle of Stalingrad
4. Mohandas Gandhi
5. Bethnal Green
6. Greer Garson
7. Oklahoma!
8. 617 Squadron, 'Dambusters'
9. Memphis Belle
10. Los Angeles
11. Colin Baker
12. Rome
13. Benito Mussolini
14. Lord Mountbatten
15. Sobibór
16. China
17. Stalin, Churchill and Roosevelt
18. Bevin Boys
19. Pigeons
20. The Great Depression

Answers

The Year That Was – 1944

1. Jimmy Page
2. Italy
3. PAYE
4. Casablanca
5. Teaching
6. Sweden
7. Mount Vesuvius
8. He bailed out of a burning Lancaster bomber without a parachute at 18,000 feet. Fir trees and deep snow broke his fall and he suffered only a sprained ankle.
9. Harry is the name of the tunnel used in The Great Escape.
10. The BBC transmitted the second line of the poem to inform the French Resistance that the invasion was about to start.
11. Operation Overlord
12. V-1 flying bomb
13. Execution
14. Iceland
15. Adolf Hitler
16. Secondary Modern, Technical and Grammar
17. Richard Austen 'Rab' Butler
18. Pipe-Lines Under The Ocean
19. Retribution Weapon 2
20. Northwest Passage

The Year That Was – 1945

1. Jacqueline du Pré
2. Crimean Peninsula
3. Raising the American flag
4. Bridgend
5. Judge
6. Bergen-Belsen
7. Cyanide
8. Ezra Pound
9. Channel Islands
10. Lord Haw-Haw
11. General Election
12. Nuclear bomb
13. Clement Attlee
14. BBC Light Programme/ Radio 2
15. Giles
16. Little Boy
17. Iron Curtain
18. George Orwell
19. Piccadilly Circus
20. Banana

The Year That Was – 1946

1. United Nations
2. Earth and the Moon
3. Charles de Gaulle
4. Electronic Numerical Integrator and Computer (ENIAC)
5. Argentina
6. Japan
7. Vespa motorcycle
8. Alcatraz Prison
9. Sony
10. H-bomb
11. Greece
12. Italy
13. Cannes
14. Bikini
15. Cathay Pacific
16. Table
17. Car radiotelephone service
18. Susan Sarandon
19. Muffin the Mule
20. The United Nations Children's Emergency Fund

The Year That Was – 1947

1. Silver
2. David Bowie
3. Al Capone
4. Severe winter weather caused power cuts and fuel shortages.
5. Lord Mountbatten
6. Ealing Comedy
7. Tom and Jerry
8. School leaving age
9. Gardeners' Question Time
10. Heligoland
11. SAAB
12. Llangollen International Musical Eisteddfod
13. Princess Elizabeth and Lt. Philip Mountbatten
14. Edinburgh Festival
15. Flying saucer
16. Kon-Tiki
17. Computer
18. He accidentally leaked a budget speech secret to a journalist.
19. Wedding of Princess Elizabeth and The Duke of Edinburgh
20. Cambridge

Answers

The Year That Was – 1948

1. Self-service
2. Ellis Powell
3. All-time highest attendance for an English Football League fixture
4. Mahatma Gandhi
5. Luxembourg and the Netherlands
6. Frank Muir and Denis Norden
7. Polo
8. Land Rover Series 1
9. Israel
10. Berlin Airlift
11. St. Fagans
12. National Health Service
13. Alcoholics Anonymous
14. Comprehensive schools
15. Lester Piggott
16. Break the sound barrier
17. Freddie Grisewood
18. Birth of Charles, future Prince of Wales
19. Bertrand Russell
20. Malcolm Campbell

The Year That Was – 1949

1. Noddy
2. National Service
3. Big Bang
4. Longleat House
5. North Atlantic Treaty
6. Badminton Horse Trials
7. Wolverhampton Wanderers
8. Neptune
9. Launderette
10. Whisky Galore!
11. Production commercial jetliner
12. Civilians
13. Atomic bomb
14. Twiggy
15. Tokyo Rose
16. Food
17. Terry Thomas
18. Cwmbran
19. Sutton Coldfield
20. The Netherlands

The Forces' Sweethearts – Betty Grable

1. 12
2. Follow the Fleet
3. Crowds
4. Million Dollar Legs
5. Ethel Merman
6. 20th Century-Fox
7. Carmen Miranda
8. I Wake Up Screaming
9. Victor Mature
10. Harry James
11. The 'Gay Nineties'
12. Standing with right hand on hip, back to camera, looking over her shoulder.
13. Pin Up Girl
14. Mother Wore Tights
15. Douglas Fairbanks, Jr.
16. Dan Dailey
17. Gentlemen Prefer Blondes
18. How to Marry a Millionaire
19. There's No Business Like Show Business
20. How to Be Very, Very Popular

Major Inventions of the Decade

1. Jacques Cousteau
2. Kidney
3. Microwave oven
4. Frisbee
5. Aerosol spray can
6. Penicillin
7. Silly Putty
8. Electronic digital programmable computer
9. Velcro®
10. M&M's
11. LSD
12. Slinky
13. Atomic Bomb
14. LEGO®
15. Tupperware
16. Scrabble
17. Transistor
18. John Logie Baird
19. Alexander Fleming
20. Jerrycan

Answers

Big Bands

1. Frank Sinatra
2. Ted Heath
3. Stanley Black
4. Count Basie
5. Tommy Dorsey
6. Gold record
7. Woody Herman
8. Billy Cotton
9. Benny Goodman
10. Charlie Parker
11. 'Take the 'A' Train'
12. Jack Hylton
13. Stan Kenton
14. Glenn Miller
15. All the members were female
16. Charlie Barnet
17. 'Stardust'
18. Ray Ellington
19. 'Pennsylvania 6-5000'
20. Muggles

George Formby

1. Wigan
2. A violent coughing fit
3. Horse racing
4. From his father, George Formby (James Lawler Booth), who was a successful music-hall comedian and singer.
5. Ukulele
6. 'When I'm Cleaning Windows'
7. Clog dancing
8. 'With My Little Stick of Blackpool Rock'
9. ENSA
10. 'When I'm Cleaning Windows'
11. Turned Out Nice Again
12. Leaning on a lamppost
13. £500,000
14. Kathleen Harrison
15. Dinah Sheridan
16. Spare a Copper
17. He Snoops to Conquer
18. 3 million
19. George in Civvy Street
20. Morphine

The Forces' Sweethearts – Rita Hayworth

1. Margarita Cansino
2. It was her mother's maiden name.
3. Joan Crawford
4. Olivia de Havilland
5. Tyrone Power
6. Fred Astaire
7. The Love Goddess
8. Gilda
9. Fred Astaire
10. Victor Mature
11. Orson Welles
12. Five
13. Cover Girl
14. The Windmill Theatre
15. Glenn Ford
16. An atomic bomb
17. Mame
18. Platinum blonde
19. Joan Fontaine
20. Salome

The Battle of Britain

1. July to October
2. Speaking in the House of Commons on 8th June, 1940, Winston Churchill declared: 'What General Weygand has called The Battle of France is over. The Battle of Britain is about to begin.'
3. Street decorations for the homecoming parades of German forces
4. False: Hurricanes outnumbered Spitfires 2:1.
5. 342 mph
6. Messerschmitt (Bf 109)
7. Four
8. Bombers
9. Heavy bombers
10. 300
11. Trained pilots
12. They weren't British
13. Radio Detection And Ranging
14. The Dowding system
15. Coastal targets and British shipping in the English Channel
16. The Victoria Cross
17. They started bombing London in the belief that the RAF had been destroyed. This allowed the RAF time to regroup.
18. 'Never in the field of human conflict was so much owed by so many to so few.'
19. 15th September
20. Operation Sea Lion

Answers

Dunkirk

1. Operation Dynamo
2. Planning took place in a disused dynamo chamber deep beneath Dover Castle.
3. 27th May, 1940
4. Nine
5. 933
6. He planned and commanded the operation.
7. Just over two weeks
8. Two stone and wooden breakwaters at the mouth of the port
9. They greatly increased the speed of evacuation
10. Isle of Man
11. It was the smallest boat to take part.
12. Dunkirk Little Ships
13. Paddle steamer
14. Hitler believed the Luftwaffe could capture the area alone.
15. They were all sunk
16. Spitfires
17. Netherlands and Poland
18. Marchioness
19. c) 338,226
20. Winston Churchill

The Ministry of Information – WWII slogans

1. victory
2. shipping; meals
3. wire
4. to it
5. forward together
6. Women's Land Army
7. children
8. pigs
9. sneezes; diseases
10. gas mask
11. diary
12. of London
13. Dig
14. open; Water; Sand; Gas mask
15. hat; talk; lives
16. Make-do; mend
17. Look out
18. humble pie; food
19. the land
20. calm; carry on

Rationing

1. Petrol
2. Bacon and sugar
3. Meat (March 1940). Eggs were rationed in June 1941.
4. Two
5. Eight
6. Green
7. Blue
8. Buff
9. Doctor Carrot
10. Potato Pete
11. 60 (plus ten extra for children)
12. White bread
13. Jam (March 1941); cheese (May 1941)
14. Biscuits (1942); sausages (1943)
15. Two
16. A fish
17. False (it was the other way round)
18. Ten
19. Four
20. 1954

Victory in Europe Day

1. 8th May, 1945
2. Tuesday
3. On the evening of 7th May
4. Karl Dönitz
5. Trafalgar Square and The Mall
6. Winston Churchill
7. Seven
8. Bunting
9. 'We want the King!'
10. Ice cream
11. Ten
12. 3.00pm
13. Bonfires
14. 'There Will Always Be an England'
15. Hugged, kissed, danced and exchanged drinks!
16. They were used to light up iconic buildings such as St Paul's Cathedral
17. 'I'm Going To Get Lit Up (When the Lights Go On In London)'
18. Burma Looms Ahead
19. 2nd September, 1945
20. Rationing

Answers

The 1948 Olympic Games

1. The Austerity Games
2. London
3. 12
4. Germany and Japan
5. USSR
6. Paris
7. Pierre de Coubertin
8. Olympic Torch Bearer who lit the flame
9. Sailing
10. The Flying Housewife
11. They were male
12. They were among the 14 countries making their first appearance.
13. Starting blocks
14. It was covered
15. The 17-year-old was the youngest person to win an Olympic track and field event.
16. Hugh Laurie
17. Desert Rats
18. Lacrosse
19. 1,000 guineas
20. 25 miles

The Forces' Sweethearts – Anne Shelton

1. Patricia Sibley
2. Bert Ambrose & His Orchestra
3. 'Lili Marlene'
4. 'I Saw Mommy Kissing Santa Claus'
5. Arthur Askey
6. Jo Shelton
7. Introducing Anne
8. Malta (the show was Calling Malta)
9. Glen Miller and His Orchestra
10. She turned down Glen Miller, whose plane disappeared on its way to France.
11. Bing Crosby
12. Going My Way
13. 'If You Ever Fall In Love Again'
14. 'Galway Bay'
15. Seven
16. 'Lay Down Your Arms (and surrender to mine)'
17. St. Bernadette (the song was 'The Village of St. Bernadette')
18. Eurovision Song Contest
19. 'Sailor'
20. Yanks

Bing Crosby

1. The Bingville Bugle
2. 'Ol' Man River'
3. Dixie Lee
4. The microphone
5. Gary Cooper
6. Clark Gable
7. Holiday Inn
8. 1941
9. The original master had become damaged because it had pressed so many singles.
10. Grace Kelly
11. Going My Way
12. The Bells of St. Mary's
13. The Country Girl
14. Dorothy Lamour
15. Road to Singapore (1940), Road to Zanzibar (1941), Road to Morocco (1942), Road to Utopia (1946), Road to Rio (1947), Road to Bali (1952), The Road to Hong Kong (1962)
16. 25 years (he was 51; she was 26)
17. Pittsburgh Pirates
18. The Adventures of Ichabod and Mr Toad
19. High Society
20. Columbo

Classic Forties Movies

1. Notorious
2. National Velvet
3. Bette Davis
4. Noël Coward
5. Cary Grant
6. Pinocchio
7. He loses the hearing in one ear.
8. The Big Sleep
9. Jean Simmons
10. Gaslight
11. Fantasia
12. How Green Was My Valley
13. Casablanca
14. The Great Dictator
15. Henry V
16. Xanadu
17. Kris Kringle
18. Bambi
19. John Wayne
20. Joan Fontaine

Answers

Saturday Afternoon Westerns

1. John Wayne
2. Dana Andrews
3. Randolph Scott
4. Robert Mitchum
5. John Wayne
6. Jane Russell
7. Bullet
8. Humphrey Bogart
9. Olivia de Havilland
10. 'Rudolph the Red-Nosed Reindeer'
11. Tex Ritter
12. Audie Murphy
13. Tom Mix
14. Montgomery Clift
15. Gunfight at the O.K. Corral
16. Roy Rogers and Dale Evans
17. The Marx Brothers
18. Tom Mix
19. Walter Brennan
20. Lust in the Dust

Famous Film Quotes

1. Hynkel (Charles Chaplin), The Great Dictator (1940)
2. Fiorello (Chico Marx), A Night at the Opera (1945)
3. Charlotte Vale (Bette Davis), Now, Voyager (1942)
4. Rick Blaine (Humphrey Bogart), Casablanca (1942)
5. Harry Lime (Orson Welles), The Third Man (1949)
6. The Second Mrs De Winter, (Joan Fontaine), Rebecca (1940)
7. Cody Jarrett (James Cagney), White Heat (1949)
8. Esther Smith (Judy Garland), Meet Me in St. Louis (1944)
9. Gold Hat (Alfonso Bedoya), The Treasure of the Sierra Madre (1948)
10. Marie 'Slim' Browning (Lauren Bacall), To Have and Have Not (1944)
11. Russell Paxton (Mischa Auer), The Lady in the Dark (1944)
12. Paula Alquist (Ingrid Bergman), Gaslight (1944)
13. Tracy Lord (Katharine Hepburn), The Philadelphia Story (1940)
14. Kane (Orson Welles), Citizen Kane (1941)
15. George M Cohan (James Cagney), Yankee Doodle Dandy (1942)
16. Mortimer Brewster (Cary Grant), Arsenic and Old Lace (1944)
17. Captain Louis Renault (Claude Rains), Casablanca (1942)
18. Fred Jesson (Cyril Raymond), Brief Encounter (1945)
19. George Bailey, (James Stewart), It's a Wonderful Life (1946)
20. Philip Marlowe (Humphrey Bogart) and Vivian (Lauren Bacall), The Big Sleep (1946)

Fashion

1. Introduction of clothes rationing
2. Norman Hartnell
3. A ban on turn-ups
4. Zips and elastic
5. Make Do and Mend
6. Slacks
7. Luminous accessories
8. The Siren Suit
9. Paint-on, liquid stockings
10. CC41, designating a 'Controlled Commodity' – a label first introduced in 1941 for Utility clothing as a means of certifying that the product met with UK austerity regulations.
11. She cropped her trademark 'peek-a-boo' long locks – too many women had been involved in workplace accidents where their long hair became entangled in machinery.
12. The tying of a turban
13. Christian Dior
14. Nylon stockings
15. A tight sausage-like upwards-turned roll of hair at the nape of the neck, designed to keep the hair of Servicewomen above the collar-line, as regulation dictated.
16. Men in the RAF; there was a perception that RAF men were more appearance-obsessed, with lashings of hair product and smarter uniforms.
17. Jacqmar scarves, which were printed with patriotic and motivational designs and slogans for the home front, the armed forces and the allies.
18. Rubenstein's iconic red lipstick, with a patriotic marketing campaign that declared it 'ideal against subdued khaki and Service blues'.
19. Shampoo
20. Make-up

Answers

Frank Sinatra

1. Boxer and firefighter
2. From a forceps delivery at birth
3. 'From the Bottom of My Heart'
4. Tommy Dorsey
5. The Mafia
6. Frank Satin
7. The Voice
8. The House I Live In
9. Perforated ear drum
10. Kathryn Grayson and Gene Kelly
11. Concept album and box set
12. Ava Gardner and Mia Farrow
13. Zeppo
14. 'People Will Say We're In Love'
15. 'New York, New York'
16. The Andrews Sisters
17. Colour bar
18. On the Town
19. Frankly Sentimental
20. Eddie Fisher

ITMA

1. It's That Man Again
2. 1949; death of its star Tommy Handley
3. Writer
4. Mrs Mopp
5. 'Can I do yer now Sir?'
6. Jack Train
7. 'I don't mind if I do'
8. Hattie Jacques
9. 'But I'm all right now'
10. Claude and Cecil
11. 'After you, Claude – No, after you Cecil'
12. Mark Time
13. Liverpudlian
14. Foaming at the Mouth
15. It's That Sand Again
16. Deepend Dan
17. Tomtopia
18. Funf
19. 'This is Funf speaking'
20. Doh!

The Forces' Sweethearts – Vera Lynn

1. Welch
2. Plumber
3. 11
4. Joe Loss Orchestra
5. Charlie Kunz
6. 'Up the Wooden Hill to Bedfordshire'
7. Bert Ambrose & His Orchestra
8. Harry Lewis
9. Sincerely Yours
10. 'Auf Wiederseh'n Sweetheart'
11. 'There'll Always Be An England'
12. 'We'll Meet Again'
13. Alice Faye
14. Hello to love
15. Virginia
16. 'My Son, My Son'
17. Venus fra Vestø
18. 'We'll Meet Again'
19. She became the oldest person to top the UK album charts.
20. The bluebird is non-migratory and not indigenous to Europe.

Name the Classic Forties Novels in Which These Characters Appear

1. The Magic Faraway Tree (Enid Blyton)
2. Darkness at Noon (Arthur Koestler)
3. For Whom the Bell Tolls (Ernest Hemingway)
4. The Stranger (Albert Camus)
5. Horton Hatches the Egg (Dr Seuss)
6. Brideshead Revisited (Evelyn Waugh)
7. The Snow Goose (Paul Gallico)
8. The Glass Bead Game (Hermann Hesse)
9. The Horse's Mouth (Joyce Cary)
10. Nineteen Eighty-Four (George Orwell)
11. The Pearl (John Steinbeck)
12. Titus Groan (Mervyn Peake)
13. Under the Volcano (Malcolm Lowry)
14. Animal Farm (George Orwell)
15. The Sheltering Sky (Paul Bowles)
16. I Capture The Castle (Dodie Smith)
17. The Lion, the Witch and the Wardrobe (C.S. Lewis)
18. The Heart of the Matter (Graham Greene)
19. The Naked and the Dead (Norman Mailer)
20. Brat Farrar (Josephine Tey)

Answers

Nat King Cole

1. Montgomery
2. Chicago
3. Baptist minister
4. 17
5. Drum
6. Earl Hines
7. King Cole Swingsters
8. 'Straighten Up and Fly Right'
9. The Orson Welles Almanac
10. 'Chestnuts roasting on an open fire'
11. Jazz at the Philharmonic
12. '(I Love You) For Sentimental Reasons'
13. '(Get Your Kicks On) Route 66'
14. just to love and be loved in return
15. 'Too Young'
16. 'Mona Lisa'
17. 'Unforgettable'
18. Circular
19. Host a variety television series
20. Natalie Cole

Opening Lines – Name That Tune

1. 'All Going Back' (George Formby)
2. 'A Nightingale Sang in Berkeley Square' (Anne Shelton/Vera Lynn)
3. 'Bei Mir Bist Du Schön' (The Andrews Sisters)
4. 'Blue Orchids' (Glenn Miller)
5. 'Lay Down Your Arms' (Anne Shelton)
6. 'The Man Who Broke the Bank at Monte Carlo' (Charles Coburn)
7. 'Stardust' (Nat King Cole/Artie Shaw)
8. 'Boogie Woogie Bugle Boy' (The Andrews Sisters)
9. 'Don't Fence Me In' (Bing Crosby)
10. 'Lover Man (Oh, Where Can You Be?)' (Billie Holiday)
11. 'Let It Snow! Let It Snow! Let It Snow!' (Vaughn Monroe)
12. 'You'll Never Know' (Dick Haymes/Frank Sinatra)
13. 'Don't Sit Under The Apple Tree' (The Andrews Sisters)
14. 'The Biggest Aspidistra In The World' (Gracie Fields)
15. 'To Each His Own' (Eddy Howard/The Ink Spots)
16. 'Why Don't You Do Right' (Peggy Lee)
17. 'Buttons and Bows' (Dinah Shore)
18. 'Stormy Weather' (Lena Horne/Billie Holiday)
19. 'Nature Boy' (Nat King Cole)
20. 'Near You' (Francis Craig and His Orchestra)

Wireless Quiz

1. Billy Cotton Band Show
2. Dick Barton – Special Agent
3. Family Favourites
4. Housewives' Choice
5. Much-Binding-in-the-Marsh
6. HMS Waterlogged
7. Studio Stand Easy
8. Sports Report
9. The Glums
10. Variety Bandbox
11. Welsh Rarebit
12. Woman's Hour
13. Arthur Askey
14. Mrs Bagwash
15. Mrs Dale's Diary
16. Appointment with Fear
17. Ray's a Laugh
18. Jon Pertwee
19. Julie Andrews
20. Will Hay

Answers

The Sporting Forties

1. Helsinki
2. Don Bradman
3. New York Yankees
4. Liverpool
5. Lou Gehrig
6. Jimmy Demaret
7. Wimbledon Men's Singles Championship
8. England and Wales
9. Yogi Berra
10. Joe DiMaggio
11. Babe Ruth
12. Seabiscuit
13. Gino Bartali
14. Joe Davis
15. Joe Louis
16. Organ
17. Grand National
18. Derby County
19. First black player in modern major league baseball.
20. Manchester United

Thirty Forties Hits – Name the singers most associated with the song

1. Red Foley
2. Glenn Miller (Marion Hutton & the Modernaires)
3. Bing Crosby & The Andrews Sisters
4. Jimmy Dorsey (Bob Eberly & Helen O'Connell)
5. Dooley Wilson
6. Guy Lombardo
7. Vaughn Monroe
8. The Andrews Sisters
9. Nat King Cole
10. Spike Jones (Carl Grayson & Willie Spicer)
11. Louis Jordan/Johnny Mercer
12. Billie Holiday
13. The Ink Spots
14. Tommy Dorsey (Frank Sinatra)
15. Dinah Shore
16. Art Mooney
17. Benny Goodman
18. Kay Kyser
19. Peggy Lee
20. Jimmy Dorsey
21. The Ink Spots
22. Frankie Laine
23. Francis Craig
24. Johnny Mercer
25. Mills Brothers
26. Al Dexter/Bing Crosby & The Andrews Sisters
27. The Merry Macs/Kay Kyser
28. Ames Brothers/Johnnie Lee Wills
29. Vaughn Monroe
30. Doris Day

Forties Hollywood Musical Lyrics: Name the Song

1. 'Lady Be Good', Lady Be Good, 1941
2. 'Birth of the Blues', Birth of the Blues, 1941
3. 'For Me and My Gal', For Me and My Gal, 1942
4. 'After You've Gone', For Me and My Gal, 1942
5. 'You Were Never Lovelier', You Were Never Lovelier, 1942
6. 'I'm Dreaming of a White Christmas', Holiday Inn, 1942
7. 'Yankee Doodle Dandy', Yankee Doodle Dandy, 1942
8. 'Make Way for Tomorrow', Cover Girl, 1944
9. 'Have Yourself a Merry Little Christmas', Meet Me in St Louis, 1944
10. 'Swinging on a Star', Going My Way, 1944
11. 'Here's to the Girls', Ziegfeld Follies, 1945
12. 'Aren't You Glad You're You', The Bells of St Mary's, 1945
13. 'If You Knew Susie', Anchors Aweigh, 1945
14. 'Blue Skies', Blue Skies, 1946
15. 'Beautiful Dreamer', The Secret Life of Walter Mitty, 1947
16. 'Be A Clown', The Pirate, 1948
17. 'In Your Easter Bonnet', Easter Parade, 1948
18. 'New York, New York', On the Town, 1949
19. 'Take Me Out to the Ball Game', Take Me Out to the Ball Game, 1949
20. 'They Can't Take That Away From Me', The Barkleys of Broadway, 1949

Answers

The Forces' Sweethearts – Jane Russell

1. Ernestine
2. A small-part touring actress
3. Chiropodist
4. Cantilever bra underwired with structural steel rods (it was so uncomfortable she fooled Hughes into thinking she was wearing his ridiculous contraption by padding her own bra).
5. Billy the Kid
6. To increase publicity and audience demand.
7. Straw
8. A revolver
9. The Board of Censors ruled that the film's concentration on her breasts was indecent.
10. Bob Hope
11. 1946
12. Young Widow
13. The Paleface
14. Calamity Jane
15. Gentlemen Prefer Blondes
16. 'Diamonds Are a Girl's Best Friend'
17. $400,000
18. Frank Sinatra, Groucho Marx
19. Robert Mitchum
20. True

Bob Hope

1. Leslie Townes Hope
2. London, UK
3. Weston-super-Mare
4. Charlie Chaplin
5. Fatty Arbuckle
6. Bob Burman
7. 'Thanks for the Memory'
8. Boxing
9. Dorothy Lamour
10. Film Noir
11. The Academy Awards
12. Richard Nixon
13. Bing Crosby
14. Joan Collins
15. True. He starred in a 1939 film that happens to share a title with the more famous 1959 film starring Jack Lemmon, Tony Curtis and Marilyn Monroe.
16. Charlie Chaplin
17. Golf
18. Marilyn Maxwell
19. Lucille Ball
20. Honorary Knighthood

Cary Grant

1. Bristol
2. Marlene Dietrich
3. Mae West
4. Katharine Hepburn
5. Leopard
6. Brontosaurus
7. The Philadelphia Story
8. All of it
9. Suspicion
10. Milk
11. Barbara Hutton
12. Arsenic and Old Lace
13. Tchaikovsky
14. Cole Porter
15. Shirley Temple
16. Notorious
17. Key
18. Monkey Business
19. Dyan Cannon
20. Alfred Hitchcock

The Forces' Sweethearts – Judy Garland

1. Frances Ethel Gumm
2. Hoagy Carmichael
3. The Wizard of Oz
4. Shirley Temple
5. His 'little hunchback'
6. Mickey Rooney
7. Death scene
8. Adult on-screen kiss
9. Artie Shaw
10. Gene Kelly
11. Presenting Lily Mars
12. Meet Me in St. Louis
13. Liza Minnelli
14. Orson Welles
15. They expected her to sing.
16. Vincent Minnelli
17. Five
18. Easter Parade
19. Ginger Rogers
20. Summer Stock

Answers

The Home Guard

1. Local Defence Volunteers
2. 65
3. They had LDV printed on them.
4. To acquire weapons
5. 1.7 million
6. Female home defence group; women weren't allowed to join the Home Guard.
7. False. Home Guard volunteers manned anti-aircraft guns and shot down many planes.
8. The Defence Medal
9. Standard issue revolver for British officers during WWI.
10. Lord Croft, the Under-Secretary of State for War attempted to justify them to Parliament.
11. German paratrooper invasion imminent
12. German paratrooper invasion in progress
13. They were to be used to signal a German invasion.
14. Improvisation
15. Noël Coward
16. The Life and Death of Colonel Blimp
17. George Formby
18. Two
19. Stanley Holloway
20. Walmington-on-Sea

Which household products were advertised using these slogans?

1. Cadbury's Milk Chocolate
2. Mars Bar
3. Cadbury's Bourn-Vita
4. Fry's Sandwich Chocolate
5. Oxydol
6. Rinso
7. Mirro
8. Vim
9. Fairy
10. Tide
11. Milk
12. Processed Peas
13. Marmite
14. Carnation Milk
15. Bovril
16. Fish Fingers
17. Bird's Custard
18. VitBe
19. Bisto
20. Chivers Jams

Which household products were advertised using these slogans II?

1. Marmite
2. Crosse & Blackwell's
3. Creamola
4. Stork
5. Kellogg's Corn Flakes
6. Fruit Salt
7. Hovis
8. Marlboro
9. Bovril
10. Ovaltine
11. Pond's
12. Anadin
13. Nivea Creme
14. Palmolive
15. Barratt shoes
16. Odo-Ro-No Cream Deodorant
17. Player's (Navy Cut)
18. Drene
19. Nescafé
20. Lipton's

Winston Churchill

1. Blenheim Palace
2. Harrow
3. Royal Military College, Sandhurst
4. 4th Queen's Own Hussars
5. He became a war correspondent.
6. Havana cigars
7. Polo
8. Oldham
9. He was now a civilian.
10. His father, Lord Randolph Churchill
11. Liberal Party
12. Clementine Hozier
13. Sterilisation
14. First Lord of the Admiralty
15. Minister of Defence
16. 65
17. Tears and sweat
18. Second Battle of El Alamein
19. Nobel Prize in Literature
20. He was declared an honorary citizen of the United States

Answers

The Home Front

1. Gas masks
2. Children who were evacuated to Britain from Franco's Spain.
3. Blackout
4. Accidents in the Blackout
5. 'Billy Brown's Own Highway Code'
6. 'Wear Something White At Night'
7. 20 mph
8. £7 or free to those who earned less than £5 a week
9. Six
10. Air Raid Precautions
11. Indoors
12. 'Where is your gas mask?'
13. Red and blue
14. The American version was designed to look like Mickey, but the UK version retained just the name.
15. Farting sound
16. Full-time employment
17. Worrals of the WAAF
18. Tommy Trinder
19. How to recognise a German paratrooper and spy
20. Demob suit

You Lucky People – Tommy Trinder

1. Chumley
2. Save a Little Sunshine
3. Googie Withers
4. Sailors Three
5. Fiddlers Three
6. He organised a successful concert party.
7. Geraldo
8. British restaurants
9. Gordon Jackson
10. Auxiliary Fire Service
11. William Hartnell
12. Fires Were Started
13. Stanley Holloway
14. Betty Warren
15. The Bells Go Down
16. Fulham
17. True
18. Australia
19. Ten shilling note
20. Sunday Night at the London Palladium

Ealing Comedies

1. Alastair Sim
2. The Lavender Hill Mob
3. Irene Worth
4. Hafoduwchbenceub-wllymarchogcoch (Shed over the cess-pit of the red knight)
5. Alec Guinness
6. Jean Simmons
7. Meredith Edwards
8. Joyce Grenfell
9. Villains
10. Alec Guinness
11. Alfred, Lord Tennyson
12. Joan Greenwood
13. Another Shore
14. Margaret Rutherford
15. By forming their own independent nation state
16. Richard Attenborough
17. A Fish Called Wanda
18. A South Sea island
19. Compton Mackenzie
20. Basil Radford

Arthur Askey

1. 'Hello playmates!'
2. Liverpool
3. 'The Bee Song'
4. Band Waggon
5. BBC Broadcasting House
6. 'Stinker' Murdoch
7. Band Waggon – a spin-off movie, picking up from where the radio show left off.
8. 'Big-Hearted Arthur'
9. Charley's (Big-Hearted) Aunt
10. Rudolf Hess – the song was entitled, 'It's really nice to see you, Mr Hess'
11. The Ghost Train
12. Back-Room Boy
13. 'The Thing-Ummy Bob'
14. Gracie Fields
15. King Arthur was a Gentleman
16. Bees in Paradise
17. 'Is your journey really necessary?'
18. Before Your Very Eyes!
19. Pete Waterman
20. Acting

Answers

The Forces' Sweethearts – Gracie Fields

1. Rochdale
2. Grace Stansfield
3. Archie Pitt
4. Sally
5. 'Sally in Our Alley'
6. Stanley Holloway
7. In My Little Bottom Drawer
8. The biggest aspidistra in the world
9. Lead me to the altar
10. 'Wish Me Luck as You Wave Me Goodbye'
11. To prevent his internment as an 'enemy alien' during WWII
12. 'Sit on My Face'
13. Harp
14. Paris Underground
15. Stage Door Canteen
16. Holy Matrimony
17. Molly and Me
18. Our Gracie's Working Party
19. Festival of Britain
20. Just Gracie

Max Miller

1. The Cheeky Chappie
2. Brighton
3. Hoots Mon! It is the only footage of Miller's stage act in existence
4. 'Mary From the Dairy'
5. '...wouldn't fall in love with me'
6. Vera Lynn, at the Holborn Empire, until it was bombed, and afterwards at the London Palladium
7. The Good Old Days
8. Asking For Trouble
9. He was the highest paid variety artist in the country, earning £1,025 a week by 1943
10. Laugh at you
11. '...give me a bad name'
12. They were too blue
13. Notebooks filled with his jokes; the audience invariably chose the blue one.
14. He would set up a rhyming joke and leave the last word to the audience's imagination.
15. Max Bygraves (born William Bygraves)
16. '...another like me'
17. Donating to charity, using his birth name rather than his stage name, especially charities for the blind, after having been temporarily blinded during the war.
18. Stan Laurel, who saw Miller's act at the Holborn Empire
19. '...kiss her goodbye'
20. East claimed Miller told a very risqué joke about an encounter on a mountain pass with a naked woman. Whether Miller ever actually told the joke remains hotly debated. Miller later passed it off as urban myth.

Laurence Olivier

1. Private Lives
2. Read books
3. Greta Garbo
4. Peggy Ashcroft
5. Vivien Leigh
6. Romeo and Juliet
7. Rebecca
8. Horatio Nelson
9. Henry V
10. Hamlet
11. Christopher Lee
12. John Gielgud, Ralph Richardson
13. Ralph Richardson
14. 39
15. Alec Guinness
16. 76
17. John Hurt
18. Vivien Leigh
19. 1947
20. The Entertainer

Answers

Laurel and Hardy

1. 'The Cuckoo Song' or 'The Dance of the Cuckoos'
2. Stan Laurel was born in Cumbria, UK and Oliver Hardy in Georgia, US
3. Tug on his hair
4. He removed the heels from his shoes
5. 'White magic'
6. He would twiddle it
7. A Chump at Oxford – towards the end of the film, he played Lord Paddington
8. Saps at Sea
9. Make any creative contribution to the directing and editing – which Stan Laurel had been routinely involved with under Roach
10. Air Raid Wardens
11. Jitterbugs
12. Zoot suits used far more material than standard, war-restricted suits.
13. Robert Mitchum
14. Because of wartime rationing and changing attitudes to waste they imposed a strict one-take approach to the filming.
15. ' . . . quietly'
16. 'D'oh'
17. John Cleese
18. ' . . . nice mess you've gotten me into'
19. Frank Skinner
20. 'I have nothing to say'

Overheard in the NAAFI – WWII Songs – Fill in the blanks

1. ball; small; Himmler's; Goebbels
2. Siegfried Line; dirty washing
3. ammunition
4. an English lane
5. Sergeant-Major; wooden bed
6. go to war; Piccadilly underground
7. a hell of a time
8. Italy; spree
9. Fred Karno's
10. an England
11. harvest moon
12. mine
13. der fuehrer's face
14. gas mask
15. Lili of the lamplight